Astronauts

Other Books in the History Makers Series:

History **MAKERS**

Astronauts

By Sheila Wyborny

Lucent Books
P.O. Box 289011, San Diego, CA 92198-9011

Library of Congress Cataloging-in-Publication Data

Wyborny, Sheila.
  Astronauts / by Sheila Wyborny.
    p. cm. — (History makers)
Includes bibliographical references and index.
Summary: Profiles the history of astronauts including Yuri Gagarin, John
Glenn, Neil Armstrong, Sally Ride, Christa McAuliffe, and Mae Jemison.
  ISBN 1-56006-648-2 (hardcover : alk. paper)
  1. Astronauts—Biography—Juvenile literature. [1. Astronauts.] I. Title.
II. Series.
  TL539 .W95 2001
  629.45'0092'2—dc21

                                                           00-009444

CONTENTS

FOREWORD

The literary form most often referred to as "multiple biography" was perfected in the first century A.D. by Plutarch, a perceptive and talented moralist and historian who hailed from the small town of Chaeronea in central Greece. His most famous work, *Parallel Lives*, consists of a long series of biographies of noteworthy ancient Greek and Roman statesmen and military leaders. Frequently, Plutarch compares a famous Greek to a famous Roman, pointing out similarities in personality and achievements. These expertly constructed and very readable tracts provided later historians and others, including playwrights like Shakespeare, with priceless information about prominent ancient personages and also inspired new generations of writers to tackle the multiple biography genre.

The Lucent History Makers series proudly carries on the venerable tradition handed down from Plutarch. Each volume in the series consists of a set of five to eight biographies of important and influential historical figures who were linked together by a common factor. In *Rulers of Ancient Rome*, for example, all the figures were generals, consuls, or emperors of either the Roman Republic or Empire; while the subjects of *Fighters Against American Slavery*, though they lived in different places and times, all shared the same goal, namely the eradication of human servitude. Mindful that politicians and military leaders are not (and never have been) the only people who shape the course of history, the editors of the series have also included representatives from a wide range of endeavors, including scientists, artists, writers, philosophers, religious leaders, and sports figures.

Each book is intended to give a range of figures—some well known, others less known; some who made a great impact on history, others who made only a small impact. For instance, by making Columbus's initial voyage possible, Spain's Queen Isabella I, featured in *Women Leaders of Nations*, helped to open up the New World to exploration and exploitation by the European powers. Unarguably, therefore, she made a major contribution to a series of events that had momentous consequences for the entire world. By contrast, Catherine II, the eighteenth-century Russian queen, and Golda Meir, the modern Israeli prime minister, did not play roles of global impact; however, their policies and actions significantly influenced the historical development of both their own countries and their regional neighbors. Regardless of their relative importance in the greater historical scheme, all of the figures chronicled in the History Makers series made contributions to posterity; and their public achievements, as well as what is known about their private lives, are presented and evaluated in light of the most recent scholarship.

In addition, each volume in the series is documented and substantiated by a wide array of primary and secondary source quotations. The primary source quotes enliven the text by presenting eyewitness views of the times and culture in which each history maker lived; while the secondary source quotes, taken from the works of respected modern scholars, offer expert elaboration and/or critical commentary. Each quote is footnoted, demonstrating to the reader exactly where biographers find their information. The footnotes also provide the reader with the means of conducting additional research. Finally, to further guide and illuminate readers, each volume in the series features photographs, two bibliographies, and a comprehensive index.

The History Makers series provides both students engaged in research and more casual readers with informative, enlightening, and entertaining overviews of individuals from a variety of circumstances, professions, and backgrounds. No doubt all of them, whether loved or hated, benevolent or cruel, constructive or destructive, will remain endlessly fascinating to each new generation seeking to identify the forces that shaped their world.

The Trailblazers

By the end of the nineteenth century, the continents had been claimed and land masses had been charted. Every sea and ocean had been sailed. What frontiers remained for the explorers of the next century? These adventurers would have to look outward, away from Earth for new territories to explore.

Toward the Heavens

One significant leap toward the heavens was taken on December 17, 1903, on the windy coast of North Carolina when a printer and bicycle maker, Orville Wright, made a twelve-second, 120-foot "hop" in a motorized flying machine. Humankind had begun to reach for the clouds. Nearly sixty years later, in 1961, that reach extended beyond Earth's atmosphere when Soviet cosmonaut Yuri Gagarin became the first human in space.

In the beginning, Gagarin and the other space pioneers were culled from the ranks of the military. These astronauts and cosmonauts were experienced test pilots. America's Space Task Group, organized in 1958 and led by aerospace scientist and engineer Dr. Robert Gilruth, defined the psychological traits that would be the hallmark of America's astronauts, and test pilots possessed all of them in abundance:

1. Willingness to accept hazards comparable to those encountered in modern research airplane flight.

2. Capacity to tolerate rigorous and severe environmental conditions.

3. Ability to react adequately under conditions of stress or emergency.[1]

These qualities, enhanced by further training, would be integrated with the requirements of the space missions themselves. For example, one of the early training program manuals states,

The capsule crew consists of one man representing the peak of physical and mental acuity, training, and mission indoctrination. Much more will be required of the crewman than is normally required of the modern aircraft test pilot. The crewman must not only observe, control, and comment upon the capsule system, but must scientifically observe and comment upon his own reaction while in a new, strange environment.[2]

From Many Beginnings to a Common Goal

The agency created to oversee America's space program, the National Aeronautics and Space Administration (NASA), had a picture of what kind of man the astronaut should be and how he should be able to perform in space. To NASA fell the task of physically training, educating, and monitoring the astronaut candidates.

Astronaut trainees undergo extensive training, both physical and psychological, and complete in-depth studies in jet propulsion, astronomy, aerodynamics, meteorology, physics, navigation, flight planning, and communications.

Although the first astronauts and cosmonauts were drawn from their respective nations' military services, over the course of forty

A test pilot undergoes G-force testing. Like test pilots, astronauts were chosen for their ability to withstand rigorous physical challenges.

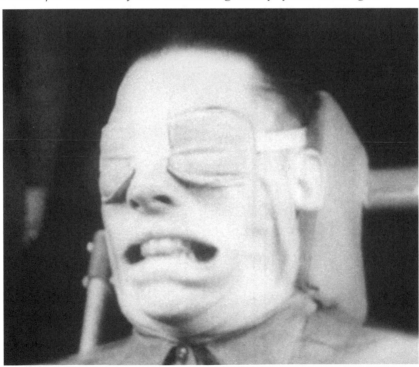

years the ranks of astronauts and cosmonauts have grown to include scientists and even ordinary citizens—female as well as male. All still undergo the same rigorous training and testing, however. And even as technology of space exploration has grown more complex over the past forty years, the basic traits sought in astronaut candidates remains the same; physical fitness, intelligence, curiosity, and courage.

Though separated by background, the space pioneers profiled here are united by the qualities that led them to reach toward the heavens. Yuri Gagarin, John Glenn, Neil Armstrong, Sally Ride, Christa McAuliffe, and Mae Jemison are six astronauts whose achievements during humankind's first forty years in space will be remembered well into the twenty-first century and beyond.

CHAPTER 1

Man in Space: From Watcher to Wanderer

In the first decades of the seventeenth century, Italian astronomer Galileo pointed a cylindrical instrument toward the heavens. He observed that the Moon was "uneven, rough, and full of cavities and prominences, being not unlike the face of Earth."[3]

For a while, it was enough to merely observe the heavens through these instruments, called telescopes, but the time came when humankind began to wonder what it would be like to reach out to these places that could only be observed from a great distance. People began to dream of space travel, and from the dreams came the visions.

The Visionaries

In the 1890s Russian scientist Konstantin Tsiolkovsky wrote *Dreams of Earth* and *Cosmic Space by Means of Reaction Devices*. In his writings, Tsiolkovsky presented a design for a multistage rocket and theorized that hydrogen and oxygen could be combined to fuel powerful rockets. He believed that space travel was a real possibility, and he came to be known as "the Father of Space Rocketry."

Rocket engineer Robert Goddard with a small rocket motor.

Thirty years later an American carried the theory of space travel several steps farther when, in 1920, the Smithsonian Institution published a paper titled *A Method of Reaching Extreme Altitudes* by Robert Goddard. Goddard described a machine that could escape Earth's atmosphere and travel into space. This rocket was not portrayed as a way for people to travel in space but rather as a means of forecasting weather by lofting a recording device higher into the sky than the twenty miles that weather balloons of that era were capable of reaching.

Over the next twenty-five years, researchers made steady progress in gaining the knowledge needed to conquer space. Much of this progress was made as scientists developed ever more destructive weapons during and immediately after World War II.

Why Space?

During more than four decades following World War II, the United States and the Soviet Union competed fiercely to gain the strategic advantage in the development of increasingly sophisticated atomic weapons. Control of outer space, American and Soviet leaders reasoned, was key to gaining this advantage. Therefore, when the Soviet Union succeeded in placing a small artificial satellite into Earth's orbit in October 1957, American military planners were alarmed. If the Soviets could manage this feat, it seemed only a matter of time before weapons of war, aimed at American cities, would be orbiting the globe.

To help develop its response to this threat from the Soviets, the United States turned to a former enemy. German physicist Werner von Braun had helped develop the first ballistic missile, the dreaded V-2, which was used against Britain late in the war. After the war, Dr. von Braun emigrated from Germany to the United States, where he dedicated his expertise to launching a satellite into orbit. Von Braun's

A model of Explorer I, *the first American satellite with its booster rocket.* Explorer I *was launched on January 31, 1958, from Cape Canaveral, Florida.*

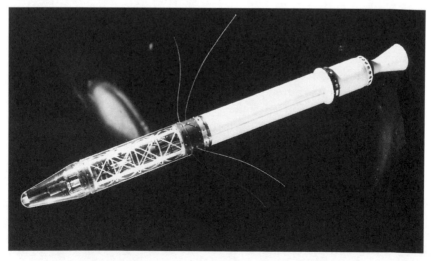

Ham, one of the first chimpanzees in space, reaches for an apple after a flight in 1961.

experience in developing rocket engines proved crucial to the eventual success of America's first satellite, *Explorer I*.

Animals in Space

By the close of the 1950s, both the Soviet Union and the United States were planning to put men in outer space. But before risking human life in space, Soviet and American scientists wanted to know how other living organisms would survive in a space environment. Thus, a number of animals were launched in small capsules atop rockets to test the reactions of their bodily functions to the rigors of space travel. The Soviets sent Laika, a female fox terrier into space in November 1957. American scientists, however, chose to send animals into space that had physiologies more like that of humans. The pioneering primates were two rhesus monkeys, Sam and Miss Sam, and too chimpanzees, Ham and Enos.

Finally, after extensive test flights with animals and a careful evaluation of the living creatures' responses to the gravitational force of launch, flight, and the return to Earth, the two rivals were nearly ready to send a human into space.

Shoot the Moon

The Soviets had already achieved two firsts in space: with *Sputnik 1* and by sending the first animal into orbit. But the USSR's ambitions were far greater. The Russians hoped that the first human to walk on the Moon would be a Soviet.

Even as they were preparing to send the first man into Earth's orbit, the Soviets launched three unmanned spacecraft toward the Moon to pave the way for a manned lunar mission. These three spacecraft, *Luna 1, 2,* and *3,* were designed to test the theories and calculations that would later come into play when the spacecraft would be carrying Soviet cosmonauts. Soviet prestige grew around the world as each of these three probes achieved its objective.

While the Soviets were enjoying one success after another, the Americans had little to cheer about. It was not until March 3, 1959, that the United States successfully launched its first lunar probe, *Pioneer 4*. The first three Pioneer launches, which were intended to provide close-up photographs of the moon, had ended in disaster. *Pioneer 4* was more successful. In addition to passing within thirty-five thousand miles of the Moon, *Pioneer 4*'s instruments determined that radiation levels in space were low enough that, with proper protection at least, astronauts would be able to survive in space. *Pioneer 4* filled a crucial gap in what scientists knew about space, bringing humankind one step closer to space travel.

Humans in Space

With the success of *Pioneer 4*, the American space program seemed to be closing the distance in the race with the Soviets to conquer space. But the United States was dealt yet another demoralizing blow when Soviet air force pilot Yuri Gagarin became the first human in space on April 12, 1961.

The United States did not lag very far behind with the flight of Alan Shepard less than a month later on May 5. Shepard's spacecraft, named *Freedom 7*, was launched atop an army Redstone rocket. Unlike Gagarin's flight, however, Shepard's was not meant to achieve orbit. Shepard traveled 304 miles down range with a time aloft of fifteen minutes, twenty-two seconds. He reached an altitude of 116 miles, which meant that he was weightless for a brief time.

Humans had achieved space flight, but the journey had barely begun. On May 25, 1961, U.S. president John F. Kennedy addressed a joint session of Congress. In his speech, he committed America to landing an astronaut on the Moon by the end of the decade.

Yuri Gagarin, the first human in space. Gagarin's April 12, 1961, flight was a major milestone for the Soviet Union in the space race.

Kennedy pointed out that he was setting for the nation a goal that was both grandiose and hard to reach: "No single space project in this period will be more exciting, or more impressive to mankind, or more important for the long range exploration of space; and none will be so difficult or expensive to accomplish."[4]

Tragedy

The United States forged ahead toward President Kennedy's goal, but achieving that goal came at a high price. The U.S. space program continued smoothly throughout the Mercury and Gemini programs, placing Americans—alone at first and then in pairs—in orbit around Earth. Projects Mercury and Gemini had gathered valuable information, but it was the Apollo program, with its three-man capsules, that had as its objective placing an astronaut on the Moon. But as preparations were made for the launch of *Apollo 1*, an accident occurred that brought not only tragedy but also lengthy delays to the U.S. space program.

On January 27, 1967, the crew of *Apollo 1* were in the midst of a training exercise in their capsule atop the *Saturn* rocket. At 6:31 P.M., the voice of astronaut Roger B. Chaffee was heard over the intercom: "Fire, I smell fire."[5]

(Left to right) Virgil I. "Gus" Grissom, Edwin H. White, and Roger B. Chaffee died in a fire aboard Apollo 1 *in 1967.*

In less than thirty seconds, fire engulfed the oxygen-enriched interior of the craft; before any rescue attempt could be made, astronauts Chaffee, Edwin H. White, and Virgil I. "Gus" Grissom were dead. Investigation revealed that the fire had been caused by a short circuit in a wire bundle under Grissom's seat.

While the United States suffered its first space-related catastrophe, the Soviet space program suffered a tragedy of its own. The same year as the *Apollo 1* fire, Soviet astronaut Vladimir Komarov died during reentry from orbit, reportedly when the parachute on his *Soyuz 1* spacecraft became snarled before it could deploy properly.

In the United States, NASA delayed future manned flights pending further ground testing and then launched several unmanned Apollo spacecraft. NASA wanted to be certain that every precaution was taken to eliminate design flaws in its spacecraft that could result in equipment damage and, more importantly, loss of life. America's next manned flight took place on October 11, 1968, with the launch of *Apollo 7*.

Triumph

It would be the *Apollo 11* mission, launched July 16, 1969, that would finally place a man on the Moon. And this time, the United States took a backseat to no one. An American astronaut was the first person to set foot on the Moon.

Although the United States had achieved the goal set by President Kennedy, it was not long before the world was reminded that space travel was not routine. As *Apollo 13* journeyed toward the Moon, a chain of events unfolded that demonstrated for everyone the dangers inherent in space exploration. The drama began with a transmission from astronauts Fred W. Haise Jr. and James A. Lovell Jr.:

Haise (to Houston Control): Hey we've got a problem here.

Houston Control: This is Houston. Say again, please.

Haise: Houston, we've had a problem. We've had a main B bus interval.

Lovell: We are venting something out into space. It's a gas of some sort.[6]

For reasons that were unclear at the time, the second oxygen tank had ruptured. The explosion had torn away a section of the outer skin of the service module, the part of the craft that was meant to remain in orbit while the lunar module landed on the Moon. Only one of *Apollo 13*'s three fuel cells was working, and even that one appeared to be in trouble. The lunar landing had to be scrubbed. In order to return safely to Earth, the astronauts were forced to rely on the life-support system in the lunar module for most of the trip back home, and then reenter the command module for reentry into Earth's atmosphere.

The United States achieved the first manned lunar landing.

The *Apollo 13* mission concluded with a successful splashdown in the Pacific Ocean. Americans were happy and relieved that the astronauts had survived the dangerous journey. Four subsequent Apollo missions landed safely on the Moon, but even before the end of the Apollo program, the American space effort was heading in a new direction.

Although Americans were proud of the achievements of their astronauts, as taxpayers they questioned the amount of money the government was spending on rockets, space capsules, and other nonreusable equipment, much of which would eventually become space junk orbiting Earth. By the early days of the 1970s, NASA had plans for using its resources more efficiently.

Recycled Spacecraft

President Richard Nixon wanted the space program to continue, despite growing concerns on the part of the American people. To do that, something would have to be done to hold down costs. In March 1970 a new program was announced, aimed at reducing waste in the exploration of space and commercializing space travel. The centerpiece of the new program was a revolutionary spacecraft called a space shuttle. Rather than being designed for a single mission, the space shuttle was meant to be launched into space and then glide back to Earth at the end of its mission, ready to be used over and over again. Not only would the craft be recyclable and have commercial potential, but because the shuttle was designed to carry passengers in addition to trained pilots, more Americans from diverse professions would also have the opportunity to travel in space and stay there for longer periods of time.

From Rivalry to Unity

In the years since the early 1970s, as the focus of America's space program shifted from exploring space to learning how to live in space for extended periods of time, the relationship between the American and Soviet programs shifted from rivalry toward cooperation. On July 17, 1992, U.S. president George Bush and Russian president Boris Yeltsin met in Washington, D.C., to sign a treaty outlining how the United States and Russia would work together to develop, build, and operate an international space station.

Over the course of the twentieth century, humans went from merely observing to exploring space. How that quest evolved is a story of real men and women striving to overcome formidable obstacles. These men and women became the pioneers of the space age, the astronauts.

CHAPTER 2

Yuri Gagarin: The Columbus of the Cosmos

In the cumbersome flight suit, the youthful good looks of twenty-seven-year-old Yuri Gagarin were well camouflaged. Now the speeches and other formalities were over and he was fastened into the seat of his spacecraft. His final conversation before blasting into the skies was with Sergei Korolev, the rocket's designer. Finally, Korolev finished his last-minute instructions and the scaffolding was removed from the side of the rocket. The checklists were completed, the rocket was ignited, and the craft was thrust toward the skies. Soviet pilot and now cosmonaut Yuri Gagarin became the first man to fly in space.

Making of a Hero

On March 19, 1934, Yuri Gagarin was born in a small wooden house on a large collective farm near the village of Klushino, about a hundred miles west of Moscow. Yuri's father, Alexi Ivanovich, was a farmer and a carpenter, and his mother, Anna Timofeyevna, worked in the farm's dairy.

When Yuri was about six years old, the daily routine of the farm was interrupted in a way that would change his life. He and his friends were playing outdoors when they saw two Russian fighter planes make an emergency landing in a field near his village. Young

Pioneering Soviet cosmonaut Yuri Gagarin.

Yuri and his friends had been impressed by the dashing figures who climbed from the disabled aircraft a few moments later, and they thought what a fine thing it would be to become fighter pilots. "We boys all wanted to be brave and handsome pilots,"[7] Gagarin recalled in an interview some years later.

Learning to fly would have to wait, however, since events were making mere survival difficult. Not long after witnessing the pilots' emergency landing, young Yuri and his family were forced to flee their village when, in 1941, Germany turned on its one-time ally and invaded Russia during World War II. Life was hard in the years that followed. His family lost their home; even Yuri's schooling was disrupted.

Following World War II, the Gagarin family returned to the Smolensk region of Russia. There, the family settled in the town of Gzatsk and Yuri was able to return to school, where he showed a special interest in math and science.

Although he still had his dreams of flying, Yuri had to be practical and pursue training that would enable him to make a living. As a result, much of his early education was vocational schooling, aimed at becoming a metalworker. With this training, a young man could support himself and a family.

Yuri Gagarin was, however, intelligent and capable, so in the early 1950s he entered the Industrial Technical College at Saratov to learn the more advanced skills of a factory technician. He had not relinquished his interest in becoming a pilot, however, and so he joined the Aero Club. With his first airplane ride, Gagarin was hooked on flying. He began flying lessons, and at the age of nineteen, Gagarin made his first solo flight. Not very tall, Gagarin had to sit on a cushion in the cockpit in order to see the runway and land properly.

Gagarin's determination to overcome such obstacles and his hard work in school impressed his teachers. In the spring of 1955 Gagarin graduated with honors as a foundryman-technician. But instead of going to work as a foundryman, he spent the summer at an aviation camp, learning to fly a Yak-18 fighter plane. Gagarin's hard work and skill as a pilot earned him an aviation scholarship. With the sponsorship and the support of one of the flight instructors in the Aero Club, Gagarin became an aviation cadet at the Orenburg Pilot Training School. After two more years of long hours and hard work, he graduated from Orenburg in 1957. At that time he intended to make his career in the Soviet air force.

Despite the long hours that Gagarin had invested in his training and now in his air force career, he knew there was more to life than work. Although Gagarin was, by all accounts, a hard working and dedicated pilot, he did enjoy a social life. He met and courted a nursing student named Valentina, or "Valya," as she was called by her friends. Gagarin and Valya married in 1957. But the newlyweds were not to have much time together during their first months of marriage.

Shortly after graduation from Orenburg, Gagarin was assigned to the Soviet Union's Arctic Fleet, based several miles inside the Arctic Circle, where he served his tour of duty as a jet pilot. During the earlier days of Gagarin's stint in the Arctic, Valya returned to nursing school and completed her education. With her nursing degree in hand, Valya joined her husband at the Arctic Fleet's base.

Throughout Gagarin's time with the Arctic Fleet, the launch of *Sputnik*, Russia's first satellite, was never far from his thoughts. He had heard rumors that a program to train cosmonauts to go into space was in the planning stages, so when the opportunity arose Gagarin applied for cosmonaut training.

Gagarin knew that cosmonaut trainees were being drawn from among the ranks of fighter pilots and that, with three years of experience in that area, he would be a good candidate. So it was that in the winter of 1959 Gagarin was selected to be in the first group of trainees at the cosmonaut training center, Zvezdniy Gordok ("Star City"). At Star City, the trainees began long days of intense

A model of the first Soviet satellite, Sputnik, *launched in 1957. Gagarin's interest in* Sputnik *led him to apply for cosmonaut training.*

and rigorous schooling, physical training, and medical testing as the Soviet Union forged ahead toward its goal of being the first nation to put a human into space. Gagarin's self-discipline and dedication were instrumental in placing him among the top 10 percent of his training group.

General Nikolai Kamanin, head of the cosmonaut team, observed not just Gagarin's discipline and dedication but also his ability to communicate in an open, friendly manner. These were the qualities he wanted for the Soviet Union's first man in space, and so General Kamanin nominated Gagarin for that honor. Kamanin's nomination was seconded by rocket design engineer Sergei Korolev who said, "I find in him an analytical mind and rare industriousness. We need profound information about outer space and I have no doubt that Gagarin will bring it."[8]

Gagarin was now the father of two daughters, and his image as a family man, along with his handsome appearance and boyish charm, were not lost on his superiors, either. They knew that the public would respond well to such a man. So with his wholesome image and the backing of Kamanin and Korolov, Gagarin's selection by the state commission to make the first manned space flight was unanimous.

A Historic Flight

On the morning of April 12, 1961, when the twenty-seven-year-old cosmonaut opened his eyes, he knew this might well be the day that he had been preparing for since he had begun his training.

Once again, Gagarin's self-discipline had served him well. Determined to be his best, both physically and mentally, Gagarin had managed, despite his excitement, to get a good night's sleep. When asked the morning of his flight if he had slept well, he answered, "Would it be right to take off if I had not rested? It was my duty to sleep, so I slept."[9]

Later on the morning of the launch, small metal sensors were attached to Gagarin's head and body with adhesive tape. These sensors would monitor his pulse, blood pressure, and other bodily functions and send the information back to technicians on the ground. Gherman Titov, who would man the flight if officials decided that Gagarin was—for any reason—unable to do so, was also fitted with the sensors. The two cosmonauts donned special long underwear that fit over the sensors and then pulled on pressure suits as a safety precaution in case pressure in the cabin failed. Finally, and with some difficulty, they put on the outer layer: coveralls of a bright orange, a color that would be easy to spot by recovery teams. Gloves, boots, and white helmets completed their gear. The letters *CCCP*, the Russian acronym for *Union of Soviet Socialist Republics,* were stamped in bright red across the fronts of their helmets. Once dressed, the two cosmonauts were transported to the Balkinour space center by bus.

Gagarin attempted to put his deepest emotions into words as he spoke to all of the people assembled at the space center who had worked to make this moment possible:

> At this instant, the whole of my life seemed to be condensed into one wonderful moment. . . . Of course I am happy. In all times and epochs the greatest happiness for Man has been to take part in new discoveries. To be the first to enter the cosmos, to engage single-handed in an unprecedented duel with nature—could one dream of anything more![10]

Gagarin took several moments to say good-bye to the team of engineers, the government officials, and a crowd of military officers before entering the elevator with chief rocket designer Korolev. Gagarin dedicated the flight to the people of a Communist society and, as a final farewell gesture, he bumped helmets with his backup pilot. After ascending the rocket, Gagarin and Korolev spent over an hour alone at the top, reviewing last-minute details be-

Yuri Gagarin prepares for his historic flight.

fore the hatch was sealed. Another hour passed, this time with the cosmonaut and his support team completing checklists, before Gagarin heard the words, "Switch to 'Go' position." He shouted, "Poyekhali! ["Off we go!"]"[11]

The rockets ignited and the three-ton, ball-shaped capsule accelerated through Earth's atmosphere atop the 125-foot-tall launch vehicle. Gagarin was forced against his seat with a force five times that of Earth's gravity, or five Gs. As the craft passed through the lower atmosphere, the covering over the capsule's

The Vostok I *before being raised on the launching pad. The ball-shaped capsule that would house Gagarin was in the nose of the craft.*

nose fell away as planned, allowing Gagarin to see the sky turn from blue to black as the craft began its orbit of Earth.

Back on the ground, Radio Moscow broadcast the successful beginning of Gagarin's flight. "The Soviet Union has successfully launched a manned spaceship-satellite into orbit around Earth. Present aboard the spaceship is the pilot-cosmonaut, Yuri Alexeyevich Gagarin, an Air Force pilot, twenty-seven years of age!"[12]

Throughout the flight, Gagarin's wife, Valya, waited anxiously with their two daughters—two-year-old Yelena, nicknamed "Lenochka," and two-month-old Galina—for word of her husband's safety. To occupy her time, Valya wrote a journal of the events in a school notebook.

Although Valya had known of Gagarin's flight ahead of time, another important woman in his life was taken completely by surprise. The event had been so shrouded in secrecy that Gagarin's own mother did not know that her son had been selected for the flight until the launch was announced on the radio.

Aboard his spacecraft, dubbed *Vostok 1*, Gagarin was kept busy with observations and tasks. About fourteen minutes after liftoff, he reported that the separation of the capsule from the carrier rocket was complete. Now he was in orbit and could see Earth from above its upper atmosphere. "On the horizon I could see the sharp contrasting orange from the light surface of the earth to the inky blackness of the sky,"[13] he commented later. He also noted that the weightlessness was very relaxing, much better than the G forces he felt during the acceleration of the launch.

As the spacecraft's designer had hoped, Gagarin filled the role of observer admirably. In addition to relaying his personal observations to his support team on the ground, Gagarin would eat during the brief flight. The food was not to satisfy hunger, however, since the flight was not long enough for him to need a meal. Eating was one of the tasks assigned to Gagarin because scientists hoped to learn what it would be like to eat in the weightlessness of space. Gagarin performed his assigned tasks with no apparent problems. Besides eating and drinking, he contributed a handwriting sample, later noting, "Handwriting did not change, though the hand was weightless. But it was necessary to hold the writing block, as otherwise it would float from the hands."[14]

During Gagarin's flight, his craft achieved a maximum altitude of 203 miles and a maximum speed of over seventeen thousand miles per hour. The 108-minute flight passed quickly, and Gagarin later recalled feeling disappointed when the time came for the retrorockets to fire and slow the capsule. Though all had gone well up to that point, difficulties occurred as Gagarin prepared to reenter Earth's atmosphere.

A view inside Gagarin's capsule. During the flight, Gagarin made observations and performed experiments on the effects of weightlessness.

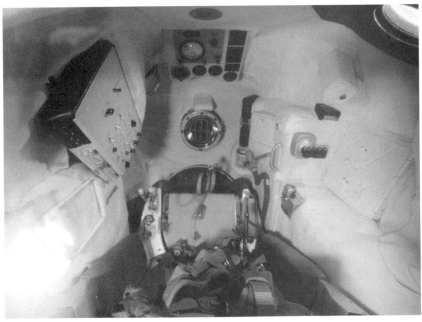

According to notes kept by Gagarin's commander at the time of his flight, Colonel Yevgeny Karpov, and which were made public some thirty-five years after the flight, *Vostok 1* began to spin out of control when the equipment module and the cosmonaut's capsule failed to separate as planned before reentry. Instead of taking ten seconds as planned, the separation took ten minutes to complete, placing Gagarin's actual landing somewhat off course from the intended landing site.

Several accounts of the end of humankind's first space journey have circulated over the years. According to one version, farmer Anya Takhtarova and her daughter were going about their daily chores when Yuri Gagarin dropped out of the sky, dangling from a parachute. Writer Peter Bond portrays the scene:

> A man wearing an orange flight suit and a white pressure helmet landed in a field watched only by a cow and the bemused peasants. As he pulled himself together and staggered to his feet, he saw the woman and a girl staring at him as he unhitched his parachute. Mrs. Takhtarova stepped toward him and doubtfully stammered, "Have you come from outer space?" To which the young man triumphantly replied, "Yes, would you believe it? I certainly have." The poor woman must have looked so frightened that he hastily added, "Don't be alarmed . . . I am Soviet!"[15]

The official account, given in 1961, is somewhat different. It states that the landing took place with Gagarin actually in the capsule. Either version is plausible, but some observers have speculated that Soviet officials wanted the flight recognized for aeronautical world records, which would not happen unless the cosmonaut returned with his craft. But regardless of the way Gagarin landed, in his capsule or apart from it, the first man in space was a national hero.

After the Adventure

Although Gagarin's flight was short, its success was crucial to the Soviet space program. His successful mission prompted the Soviet government to pump more money into the space program during the years following his flight.

As general Kamanin speculated, Gagarin proved that he had been a good choice for the first man in space. His image as a devoted family man and also a dedicated professional made him an excellent goodwill ambassador for the Soviet Union in the months following the flight. In addition to being a successful cosmonaut, he also knew how to communicate with the public so as to portray the Soviet space program in the best possible terms, enhancing the Soviet image abroad. And as a legitimate hero, Gagarin provided a big boost for the morale of his countrymen back in the Soviet Union.

Gagarin's enthusiasm for the space program and his belief that Soviet space vehicles would one day travel great distances were apparent whenever he spoke publicly, as was his patriotism. He was especially pleased that the Soviet Union had been first in space and that he had been the one to represent his homeland. "I am boundlessly happy that my beloved homeland was the first to accomplish this flight, was the first to reach outer space."[16]

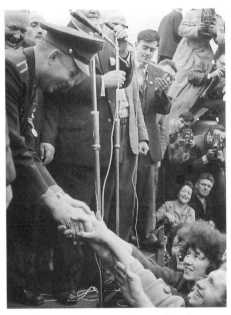

Gagarin shakes hands with admirers while on tour following his flight.

Gagarin also displayed a flair for diplomacy in his comments to the press. Following his flight, he told reporters that he favored the peaceful use of space and a peaceful competition between the superpowers. He also added that he would be happy for the American astronauts when they, too, had successful flights. "There is space for all in the universe,"[17] he said. This generosity toward his Western competitors, in addition to Gagarin's family image, also made him a favorite with the press.

Shortly after Gagarin became Earth's first man in space, he went on a world tour during which he gave speeches describing his experiences. Gagarin's quick wit and down-to-earth humility earned him many allies among the legions of otherwise hard-nosed journalists. Gagarin's charm disarmed even those who asked politically motivated questions. Once, for example, when reporters followed him into a toy store during a visit Gagarin made to Japan, a journalist asked him if he wanted to buy Japanese toys because he could not buy nice toys back in the Soviet Union. Gagarin's answer, accompanied by a friendly smile, parried the reporter's thrust: "I wanted to surprise my daughters. Now this will be all over the newspapers and it'll take away their surprise."[18]

Gagarin's personal warmth and generous spirit added to his popularity. In fact, he received so many letters asking for help with everything from better housing and health care to judicial clemency that, in addition to being assigned two assistants to help him with the barrage of mail, he was given his own postal code, Moscow 705.

Eventually Gagarin translated his personal popularity into political power. He became a deputy in his nation's legislature, the Supreme Soviet, representing his home region of Smolensk. As a legislator he attempted to use his fame and the influence that went with it among government officials to fulfill some of the requests his countrymen made of him.

Gagarin was a busy man in the years after his flight, but he continued to keep a close watch on the Soviet Union's space program. By 1967 Gagarin had become deputy director of cosmonaut training, even as he maintained his status as an active cosmonaut. He was appointed backup pilot for a flight by cosmonaut Vladimir Komarov. Gagarin had read reports of many flaws and errors in the craft, including a faulty parachute, and knew there was a high probability that the cosmonaut would not survive the mission. Unfortunately, Gagarin's fears proved true. Komarov was killed when the craft became tangled in its parachute and hurtled to the ground in an uncontrolled reentry.

Despite this accident Gagarin, who was tired of his celebrity role, wanted to return to space. As he put it, "Being a cosmonaut is my profession, and I did not choose it just to make the first flight and then give it up."[19]

A Price to Be Paid

Gagarin continued his training as he awaited his opportunity to return to space, but that dream ended on March 27, 1968. While on a routine training flight in a two-seater jet with his instructor, their aircraft crashed into a dense forest, exploding in a ball of fire. Gagarin, age thirty-four, and his instructor were both killed in the fiery crash. Gagarin's ashes were buried in the Kremlin Wall with those of other Soviet heroes.

At the time of his death in 1968, Gagarin had been polishing a speech he was to make before the United Nations that November. Gagarin had intended to pay tribute to the sacrifices of those who died to advance human knowledge. A draft of his address read in part,

> Mankind has to pay dearly for the many achievements that promote progress, frequently with the lives of its finest sons. But the advance along the path of progress is

Gagarin's widow Valya touches a portrait of her husband beneath a memorial plate on the Kremlin wall, where his ashes were interred.

inexorable. The banner of scientific achievement is picked up by others, and, true to the memory of their comrades, they march onward. For there is no greater happiness than to serve others.[20]

Gagarin continues to be remembered by his countrymen and by his colleagues in space exploration. The historic landing site of *Vostok 1* is now marked by a 130-foot-high titanium monument. Each year, thousands of visitors travel to the site to pay their respects to Gagarin. A Yuri Gagarin memorial was erected in his hometown of Saratov, and the first airplane he ever flew is on display at the Museum of Local Lore. There is a Yuri Gagarin square in central Moscow, and a bronze statue of Gagarin welcomes visitors to the cosmonauts' training center in Star City.

Yuri Gagarin's generosity with his American counterparts was rewarded in 1969, when a Yuri Gagarin commemorative medal was left on the surface of the Moon by U.S. astronaut Neil Armstrong. However far future space travel takes humankind though, Yuri Gagarin, a humble peasant's son, will be remembered as the first man in space.

CHAPTER 3

John Glenn: Grandpa in Space

On a February day in 1962, John Glenn climbed into his space capsule, *Friendship 7*. Having endured the disappointment of being passed over twice, he would shortly become the third American in space. But unknown to Glenn and his support team, Glenn would not just be experiencing the ride and leaving the actual flying of the craft to the automatic control system. Glenn was destined to become the first American to actually pilot a craft in space.

Early Years

On July 18, 1921, a red-headed, nine-pound baby boy was born to the Scottish-Irish Glenn family of Cambridge, Ohio. His parents named him John Herschel Glenn Jr., but he soon picked up the nickname "Bud."

And from his earliest years, Bud Glenn loved airplanes. "They'd spread their arms out like wings and go 'zzzoooomm' as they ran around, dipping their arms as they banked for a turn,"[21] recalled John Glenn's father, speaking of his earliest recollections of his son's childhood games.

Bud's interest in aircraft continued throughout his childhood. Like many young boys, Bud enjoyed building model airplanes, the parts cut out of sheets of balsa wood. Later as a teenager, Bud would plead with his father to take him to air shows. Because his father was as fascinated by airplanes as Bud was, it took little persuasion; the Cleveland Air Races became an annual outing for father and son.

The Dating Game

Following his graduation from high school, Bud Glenn attended Muskingum College in New Concord, Ohio. A small community, New Concord was the sort of place where everyone knew what everyone else was doing. In such an environment, it was difficult for Muskingum students to stray far from the moral code imposed by the town's older residents. In fact, New Concord had such a straight-laced reputation that conductors on the railroad that ran through town nicknamed it "Saint's Rest."

At Muskingum College, students attended mandatory chapel and observed strictly enforced curfews. The students were not allowed to have automobiles for fear they might travel to places like nearby Zanesville, where saloons beckoned. Smoking, on or off campus, was enough to get a student suspended. Yet despite the repressive atmosphere of the small community, Glenn managed a courtship with a young woman he had been in love with since early childhood, Annie Castor.

Muskingum and New Concord had strict rules governing most behavior, but there was no rule against Bud Glenn pursuing his other love, flying. So Glenn took flying lessons in his spare time, and when he was barely twenty years old, he earned his pilot's license on July 1, 1941. An even more momentous event occurred just a few months later, one that would alter the future for millions of young men and women around the world.

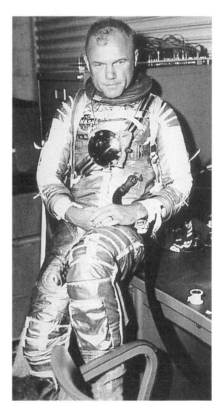

John Glenn in his spacesuit before his 1962 flight.

Military Experiences

On December 7, 1941, Japan attacked Pearl Harbor, home to the American navy's Pacific Fleet. The attack resulted in the United States becoming fully involved in World War II. Like many young men his age, Glenn left college and enlisted in the armed forces.

Glenn had already decided that he would make a career in aviation, so he dropped out of college and enlisted in the Naval Air Cadet Program. In 1943 Glenn received his commission in the Marine Corps and was sent to the South Pacific.

Glenn was trained to be a bomber pilot. But rather than drop bombs from the relative safety of high altitudes, Glenn flew a dive-bomber, which brought him down close to the enemy's positions. On one such mission, Glenn flew a pass at an altitude of fifteen feet. As he prepared to climb, he took a ninety millimeter shell in his plane's tail section, which damaged the elevators, the part of the tail that controls the ascent and descent of the aircraft. With strength born of desperation, Glenn was able to force the controls enough to control the aircraft. When he returned to his base, mechanics discovered over 250 holes in the plane. The extensive damage from the enemy's flak earned Glenn his second nickname, "Old Magnet Tail."

Prior to shipping out for the South Pacific, Glenn had married his childhood sweetheart, Annie. With the war's end came the birth of the Glenns' first child, David, in 1945. A daughter, Lynn, was born two years later, in 1947. Glenn had a family, but he was not destined to have time to spend at home right away.

World War II had barely ended when war broke out in Korea. Glenn had remained in the marines, so once again he flew into combat. By the time the Korean War ended, Glen had flown 149 missions in two wars. Glenn's service left him a highly decorated combat pilot. These honors included the Distinguished Flying Cross, which he was awarded on six occasions, and the Air Medal

A dive-bomber like the one flown by John Glenn fires its rockets. The dive-bombers Glenn flew during World War II could fire rockets as well as drop bombs.

Test pilots (pictured) flew new and experimental aircraft. The thrill and potential to learn from flying these aircraft appealed to Glenn.

with eighteen clusters, meaning that he had been given the Air Medal an additional eighteen times.

From Combat Pilot to Test Pilot

Following the war and his action in Korea, Glenn wanted to continue his service in the marines, and saw that he could best do that as a test pilot, flying new or experimental aircraft to see that they perform correctly under a wide variety of conditions. For Glenn, this was an opportunity to continually improve his flying skills and to enjoy the thrill of piloting state-of-the-art aircraft.

Because it involves pushing them up to—and often beyond—the limits they are designed for, testing new aircraft can be quite dangerous, and Glenn experienced several close calls. During one test flight, for instance, a large portion of the wing tip of his aircraft broke away. Instead of making an emergency landing, Glenn continued the flight to see how the plane would perform under these conditions. Then he safely landed the aircraft.

Before he could even get a chance to test his skills against experimental airplanes, Glenn had another obstacle to overcome and he very nearly failed to even make it into the test pilot program. It wasn't enough to fly the airplanes. Test pilots were required to be proficient in complex mathematical calculations, and because he had not taken calculus in college, Glenn was deficient in that area. Most of the other test pilots were graduates of prestigious U.S. Naval Academy, where calculus and other math and engineering courses were required. Now it would be Glenn strength of will that would make the difference.

The Naval Air Test Station at Patuxent, Maryland, or Pax River as it was known locally, was considered a prime opportunity for a pilot to further his career, and Glenn's superiors knew that Glenn's ambition and ability to overcome obstacles by sheer determination and effort would give him an edge. They felt that he could overcome his math deficiencies, and they recommended Glenn for a position at Pax River.

Earning and keeping his position would require all of his concentration during his period of training. Since he knew that his work and study hours would reach far into the night, Glenn felt it was best if his wife, Annie, and the children remain back in Ohio, near both of their families. As expected, he found the math hard. Glenn often had his lights on until after three in the morning, struggling with calculus. Despite the difficulties, Glenn completed his coursework and graduated from the Pax River program as a marine test pilot in August 1954.

Breaking Sound Barriers and Speed Records

Upon graduation from Pax River, one of Glenn's first assignments was to test the Crusader, a very sleek, fast, state-of-the-art jet. It had passed all the tests except one. The aircraft would be flown at top speed over a long distance to test its endurance. Glenn was chosen to fly the Crusader for this final test. He took off from California on July 16, 1957. Glenn landed in New York 3 hours, 23 minutes, 8.4 seconds after takeoff. He had set a new coast-to-coast speed record: an average of three thousand feet per second. Glenn returned to his hometown a hero amid parades, ceremonies, and banquets.

America's First Astronauts

A hometown boy had made a name for himself, but Glenn was destined to achieve even greater recognition. Not long after his record-breaking flight, the National Aeronautics and Space Administration (NASA) was formed. Shortly thereafter it created Project Mercury, with the objective of putting Americans in space. When Glenn heard about the program, he wanted to become a part of it, but once again, the path toward his goal was littered with obstacles. This time the difficulties went beyond his educational limitations and would test even John Glenn's well-known will of iron.

NASA had very specific guidelines for choosing candidates for its astronaut corps. First, at 208 pounds, Glenn would be considered overweight for the program. Secondly, the maximum allow-

able height was five feet and eleven and a half inches. Glenn was six feet tall. NASA also wanted its astronauts to be college graduates. Although he had completed enough hours to graduate, Glenn did not actually hold a college degree. Finally, the cutoff age for astronauts was thirty-nine. Since Glenn was already thirty-seven when he applied, he would be near the maximum age by the time he completed all of his training.

Glenn attacked the physical requirements first. For a couple of hours each evening, he strapped books to his head in an effort to compress his spine and shrink the necessary half inch. Glenn tackled the weight problem with equal zeal, determined to lose more than forty pounds.

By the time he completed his strict diet regimen, Glenn, sunken-cheeked and hollow-eyed, looked like an escaped prisoner of war, but he had achieved the weight limit. He had also managed to squeeze by the height requirement as well and was now at the requisite five feet eleven and a half inches. But the issue of the college degree, or lack of one, was another matter.

Luckily, Glenn had a champion in his corner. Marine colonel Jake Dillon, Glenn's commanding officer at Pax River, was determined

Glenn in the Crusader's cockpit. Glenn flew the Crusader from California to New York, setting a new coast-to-coast speed record.

that a marine should be included in the first group of astronauts. Moreover, he wanted Glenn to be that marine. NASA's requirements contained a loophole, in that the equivalent of a bachelor's degree was acceptable, so with Colonel Dillon's backing, NASA accepted the courses Glenn had taken in college and following World War II through the Armed Forces Institute, plus his Pax River courses, as being equivalent to a college degree.

To Glenn's dismay, Alan Shepard (pictured) was chosen to be the first American in space.

Glenn had been accepted as one of the first seven astronauts, but he was prevented from achieving his next goal: being the first American in Space. Glenn was stunned when he learned that Alan Shepard, not he, would be America's, if not the world's, first man in space. Glenn genuinely believed that he deserved the honor of being first, and he greatly resented NASA's decision. Biographer Frank Van Riper notes that Glenn took being passed over badly:

> The most highly decorated of all of the astronauts, the most record-breaking test pilot, the candidate who breezed through the testing at Lovelace and Wright-Pat [Wright Patterson Air Force Base] was being passed over for Alan Shepard. The fact that Shepard's test scores had also been superb, in fact higher than Glenn's in the critically important procedures training, would, as Glenn later reflected, assuage his grievously wounded ego. But for now Glenn had only his rage.[22]

What frustrated Glenn was that he could do absolutely nothing to affect NASA's selection process. Up to this point, Glenn had sometimes been able to pull strings in order to overcome obstacles, but this time nothing could influence NASA's administrators because the decision had been announced publicly.

Glenn turned his anger on those closest to him. He became sullen and withdrawn from his wife, Annie, and his children, David and Lynn. His friend Tom Miller finally got fed up with Glenn's attitude one day and took him to task: "We were out in the yard together and I called him every name I could think of, the nicest being selfish. 'You may hate me for this,' I told him, 'but I think you're wrecking your family and yourself. You don't know when you're well off! Now get off of it, dammit!'"[23] Glenn realized that his friend was right and that his behavior had been making the people who cared about him the most miserable. He still was not happy about NASA's decision, but Glenn began making an effort not to take out his disappointment on his friends and family.

Yet another disappointment awaited Glenn. When the second American spaceman was chosen, Glenn was passed over again, this time in favor of Gus Grissom. John Glenn would have to settle for being the third American in space. There was one consolation for being third in line, however. Whereas Shepard's and Grissom's flights had been suborbital, Glenn's mission would make several orbits of Earth.

Friendship 7

Glenn's adventure began at 9:47 on the morning of February 20, 1962. Inside his capsule, *Friendship 7*, Glenn lifted off from Florida's Cape Canaveral Launch Complex 14. The flight was anything but smooth. Shortly after launch, as the rocket rolled into position on its orbital trajectory, the craft began to vibrate. As the Atlas rocket on which the *Mercury* capsule was mounted broke the sound barrier, the vibrations worsened, the noise almost drowning out the engines' roar. After about two minutes, as planned, two of

Glenn is helped into Friendship 7 *(left) and lifts off (right) on February 20, 1962.*

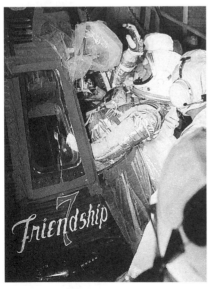 

the booster engines of the rocket shut down, and Glenn was violently jerked forward in his seat. The redundant, or supporting, rockets had separated and slid away. Now the craft pitched downward, giving Glenn his first look back at Earth. The horizon was sharply defined against the darkness of space. Then the main rocket booster ignited and accelerated the craft to its orbital velocity of 17,500 miles per hour. Once orbit had been achieved, the rocket booster shut off and was jettisoned, and Glenn was weightless. Five-and-a-half minutes into the flight, he was cleared by Mission Control for at least seven orbits.

Thirty-eight minutes after the launch, Glenn experienced his first passage to the nighttime segment of an orbit. He reported what he saw to those back on Earth: "Orbital sunset is tremendous . . . a truly beautiful and remarkable sight."[24]

Half an hour after witnessing the spectacular sunset, Glenn had an unexpected experience. As he watched the sunrise behind him through a periscope, a swarm of bright, yellowish-green specks surrounded the capsule. "It was as though I were walking backward through a field of fireflies,"[25] he reported to Mission Control. After a while, as the sunrise continued, these "space needles" gradually disappeared. The space needles were later named "the Glenn Effect" by NASA scientists because Glenn remains the only astronaut to have ever observed this phenomenon.

Although the space needles caused no problems, other difficulties soon arose. Nearly an hour and a half into the flight, a small thruster stuck in the "on" position and Glenn had to override the automatic control systems and pilot the craft himself to keep *Friendship 7* at the correct attitude, or angle. Then, as NASA officials were carefully tracking Glenn's progress into his second orbit, one of their instruments indicated that the capsule's landing bag had been released early.

The landing bag had a crucial function. It was made of a rubberized glass material that, once deployed, extended four feet beyond the base of the capsule. It was designed to cushion the craft during the impact of splashdown by pushing the heat shield away from the rear of the capsule. Controllers feared that the heat shield, which was needed to protect the capsule and its occupant from the heat generated by reentering the atmosphere, might now break loose from the craft. Without the heat shield, the capsule and its occupant would burn up during reentry. Controllers ordered Glenn to keep his landing bag switch in the "off" position, and then reminded him of this directive six minutes later when they asked if he had heard any banging or flapping noises. He had heard none, but he began to wonder about the import of the questions he was receiving from the ground.

Despite the problems, Glenn was confident he could complete at least three orbits, and Mission Control gave its approval. Finally, when Glenn was preparing for reentry, he was told the reason for the questions controllers had been asking. Now came the moment of truth. He would have to turn on the landing bag switch. If the green light came on, that would mean the landing bag had already deployed.

Glenn flipped the switch and there was no green light. If his instruments were right and the instrument on the ground was wrong, the landing bag had not deployed. Although everyone on the ground was relieved, some doubt remained since the meter on the ground still indicated a problem.

As the capsule reentered the atmosphere, the temperature on the bottom of the craft reached sixteen hundred degrees Celsius. Scientists knew that under these conditions, radio signals would be disrupted; for four and a half minutes, Mission Control was out of contact with the capsule and its occupant. Then the craft's main parachute deployed at 10,800 feet and the landing bag that the technicians had worried about worked perfectly. *Friendship 7*, with Glenn inside, landed in the Atlantic Ocean, bobbing on the surface like a charred cork.

After Friendship 7

Although John Glenn was not the first American in space, the honors that followed his safe return were some consolation. Shortly after he was picked up by the naval destroyer *Noa*, President John F. Kennedy called him to offer his congratulations. At that same moment, the U.S. Postal Service issued the Project Mercury four-cent stamp, which had been secretly printed but held back until the safe completion of Glenn's flight. Three days after his phone call, President Kennedy came to Cape Canaveral to personally present Glenn with the Distinguished Service Medal.

Now Glenn was famous. The American public clamored for a look at their newest hero, and many parades and ceremonies followed Glenn's safe return. There was a jubilant procession through the streets of Washington, D.C., ending at the White

President John F. Kennedy pins the Distinguished Service Medal on John Glenn after the astronaut's successful flight.

House. New York City welcomed Glenn and his fellow astronauts with a tickertape parade.

Beyond being the first American in orbit, Glenn had made history in another way. Glenn's actual piloting of the craft, although accidental, had been a first. By controlling his craft for two-thirds of his mission, Glenn had shown America and the rest of the world that astronauts need not be mere passengers in a craft controlled by automatic systems—they could be actual space pilots.

For two years following his spaceflight, Glenn remained with NASA and the U.S. Marine Corps. But then Glenn was ready for a new challenge. In 1964 he resigned from the marines in order to run for one of Ohio's seats in the U.S. Senate. This first attempt at public office failed, however. Because Glenn paid his campaign debts out of his own pocket, he needed money. Fortunately, many large corporations were anxious to have their name associated with that of a national hero like John Glenn.

Among the corporations seeking Glenn's attention were Royal Crown, the soft drink company, Holiday Inn, and the Ohio-based Questor Corporation. Although several corporations would have been happy to use his name, Royal Crown offered Glenn a real job as a hands-on, full-time, decision-making executive. This became a long and mutually profitable association. In addition to working for Royal Crown, Glenn also served on the board of directors of Questor, a manufacturer of auto parts, among other products. Finally, Glenn became involved with a Holiday Inn franchise in Orlando, Florida, that prospered when Disney World opened nearby a few years later.

Glenn was a successful businessman, and his investments had made him a millionaire, but the political arena continued to attract him. In 1974 Glenn once again ran for the U.S. Senate, and this time he was successful. He was reelected three more times, becoming the first senator from Ohio to win four consecutive terms.

A Trailblazer Returns

Glenn had been a success as an astronaut, as a businessman, and as a politician. He could have retired and looked back on his glory days, but at seventy-seven, he was ready to shoot for the stars one more time.

On October 29, 1998, seventy-seven-year-old John Glenn joined the crew of the space shuttle *Discovery* for a nine-day mission. The fact that the rest of the crew were young enough to be his children prompted jokes about his age. Despite the jokes, there was genuine concern about the effects that space travel might have on the body of a person Glenn's age. Speaking from space, Glenn felt otherwise: "I guess it's an advantage up here for older folks, because in zero G [gravity] you can move around much more easily."[26]

Glenn (far right) with fellow Discovery *crew members. In 1998, at age seventy-seven, Glenn completed his second space mission.*

During the flight, Glenn participated in an experiment called OSTEO, which showed how bone cells in the body respond to the weightlessness of space. The purpose of this experiment was to determine if space travel would have a positive effect on people with degenerative conditions such as loss of bone density associated with aging.

On November 7, 1998, *Discovery* touched down. Whereas Glenn's first mission completed three orbits of Earth, *Discovery* had completed 134. Glenn emerged from the craft weak after nine days of weightlessness, but smiling.

On his first mission, Glenn had proven that a person could pilot a craft in space. On his second mission he proved that older people have contributions to make to humankind's continuing quest for knowledge about what lies beyond Earth's atmosphere.

As Glenn nears eighty, he maintains a schedule that would tire men many years his junior. He makes many personal appearances each year, further reinforcing his contention that space exploration is for all people, regardless of age.

CHAPTER 4

Neil Armstrong: A Giant Leap for Mankind

On July 20, 1969, Neil Armstrong's boot made the first footprint on the surface of the Moon. A few minutes later he would be joined by fellow astronaut Edwin A. "Buzz" Aldrin Jr., but for this moment, Armstrong stood alone, the first man to view the Moon's barren, rocky terrain firsthand.

A Journey Begins in Middle America

Neil Armstrong was born on August 5, 1930, in his grandparents' farmhouse, located five miles outside of Wapakoneta, Ohio, a small community about sixty miles north of Dayton. The first of three children, he was followed by a sister, June, and then a brother, Dan.

As a small child, Neil was mesmerized by airplanes. His father, Stephen, took him to the airport when Neil was a toddler. Two-year-old Neil stood quietly and watched the airplanes take off and land, captivated by what he saw.

Neil's father was an accountant who specialized in auditing the finances of county governments, and as a consequence, the family moved frequently around the state, living in similarly furnished apart-

Neil Armstrong, the first person on the Moon.

ments wherever they went. Because they had to move so frequently, the Armstrong family traveled light, so little Neil did not have much in the way of toys. His family's frequent moves also made forming friendships with other children difficult, so Neil developed as a shy child who got his enjoyment from reading.

Neil badly wanted to fly in the airplanes that fascinated him, and his father knew that, but money was always tight and an airplane ride would be an unnecessary expense. However, when Neil was six, his father learned that the airport near where they were living offered cheaper airplane rides on Sunday than during the rest of the week, so Neil and his father played hooky from Sunday school one morning and drove to the airport. Neil took his first airplane ride in a Ford trimotor. "Neil enjoyed it tremendously, but I was scared,"[27] his father said years later.

Like many youngsters, Neil indulged his fascination with airplanes by building models, starting when he was eight years old. He wanted to earn money to build bigger and better models, so when he was old enough, Neil got his first part-time job, mowing the grass at the cemetery near where the family was living. Throughout the rest of his childhood, Neil worked a number of odd jobs.

Neil's life changed when he entered high school and his father got a position with Ohio's Department of Public Welfare. Now, instead of having to move every few months, the family was finally able to settle into a real home. They bought a house in Wapakoneta, the same town where Neil had been born. Neil, although still quiet and shy, now had the opportunity to make friends.

One friend that Neil made was a neighbor, Jacob Zints. Jacob was an amateur astronomer, and he and Neil would take a telescope to the roof of his garage and look at the Moon and planets. The whole universe now opened up for Neil.

Although busy with new friends and with activities like playing in his school's band, Neil continued to work at a variety of part-time jobs. One of those jobs was clerking at a pharmacy. He was still interested in airplanes, but now instead of spending all of his money on models, Neil was pursuing the real thing: He was saving his money to pay for flying lessons.

Charles Babcock, his boss at the pharmacy, recalled young Armstrong's interest in flying: "Neil never bothered reading comic books. Every day he would check the magazine rack to see if any new flying magazines had come in for him to read."[28]

By careful saving, it was not long before Neil was able to begin his flying lessons. In fact, he could fly an airplane before he could drive a car. The airport was located three miles outside of Wapakoneta, and after work Neil would hitchhike there for his flying lessons, which cost nine dollars each. To help pay for his lessons, Neil worked at washing airplanes and doing general cleanup around the hangars.

Although he was now involved with real airplanes, Neil maintained an interest in model aircraft as well. He took his hobby seriously, even to the point of building a wind tunnel in the basement in order to test the aerodynamic properties of some of his larger models.

Neil continued his flying lessons, and on his sixteenth birthday he earned his private pilot's license. Never a boastful person, he told none of his friends at school about this major milestone in his life, so most of them did not know that they had a real pilot in their midst. Being a pilot would certainly have gained Neil attention from girls, but he was still shy and declined to take advantage of his new status. Luckily for young Armstrong, dating was something of a group activity that did not require a boy to approach a particular girl and ask for a date. "We all dated, but there were no steadies. We went in groups, because you could only get the family car once a week. But usually we would just walk a girl home from a school or church activity,"[29] Armstrong recalled.

Model airplanes were a favorite hobby for Neil Armstrong, who maintained his interest in model planes even after he learned to fly real ones.

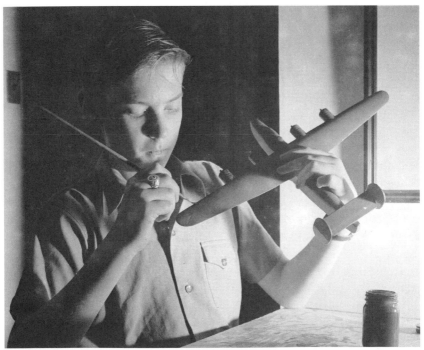

Neil graduated from high school in 1947, when he was only sixteen. He knew his parents could not afford to send him to college, so he took advantage of a scholarship program offered by the navy to attend Purdue University at West Lafayette, Indiana. Neil's plan was to major in aeronautical engineering so that he could one day design aircraft. Although he looked forward to going to college, Neil understood that, under the terms of the scholarship, the navy could call him to active duty at any time, whether or not he had finished college.

Military Years

After three years at Purdue, the navy did call Armstrong to active duty, assigning him to flight school in Pensacola, Florida. Because he was only twenty, Armstrong felt he was much too young to accept the responsibility of commanding a flight crew, so he trained in single-engine fighters.

In 1951 Armstrong's navy squadron was sent into combat in Korea, where Armstrong and his fellow pilots flew Panther jets from the aircraft carrier *Essex*. During the time he was assigned there, Armstrong flew seventy-eight combat missions and in the process accumulated three air medals. Still not one to showcase his accomplishments, Armstrong was modest when asked about the awards years later, saying, "They handed out medals like gold stars at Sunday school."[30]

During his active duty in Korea, Armstrong experienced some close calls. In one instance, Armstrong had to bail out when his aircraft was hit by enemy fire. A few months later, part of the wing of the aircraft he was flying was torn off by a North Korean booby trap in the form of a wire strung across a narrow valley that airplanes had to fly through. Despite the damage to his airplane, Armstrong was able to fly it safely back to the carrier.

Back to Civilian Life

Once his tour of duty in Korea was completed, in the fall of 1952, Armstrong returned to Purdue University to complete his degree in aeronautical engineering. In addition, he became involved in several organizations that he felt would help further his goals. He joined the American Rocket Society, the Aero Club, and became a student member of the Institute of Aeronautical Sciences. But Armstrong did not spend all his time in academic pursuits.

One day, Armstrong met pretty, dark-haired Jan Shearon, a home economics major from Evanston, Illinois, who, to Armstrong's delight, had an interest in flying. Her father had owned a

Armstrong flew Panther jets similar to this one during the Korean War, carrying out seventy-eight combat missions and earning three medals.

small plane, and her mother and her sisters had all taken flying lessons. Still shy, it was months before Armstrong worked up the courage to ask her out. Once the ice was broken, though, they continued to date for the rest of their time in college.

Armstrong earned his bachelor of science degree in aeronautical engineering in January 1955. After he and Shearon were married in 1956, he went to work for the National Advisory Committee for Aeronautics at Edwards Air Force Base in California, testing high-speed aircraft.

Neil and Jan's marriage came in for some testing of its own as they moved into a cabin in the San Gabriel Mountains, northeast of Los Angeles. Located at an elevation of five thousand feet, with no electricity and no hot water, the cabin was anything but home-like. Their marriage survived its discomfort, though, and in 1957 a son, Eric "Ricky" was born. He was followed in 1959 by a daughter, Karen.

While Jan looked after the children, Armstrong continued flying experimental aircraft. In November 1960 Armstrong made his first test flight in the X-15 rocket plane, which was designed to fly to the upper reaches of Earth's atmosphere. At this point, he was aware of, but not particularly interested in, the astronaut program. Armstrong was convinced that spacecraft like those used by NASA were not the best approach to spaceflight. In his view astronauts, sealed in their wingless space capsules, were "spam in a can," merely along for the ride. To Armstrong it seemed that the air force's Dyna-Soar project, a program to send a winged vehicle into space, had more of a future. So Armstrong added work on Dyna-Soar to his work on the X-15.

The Dyna-Soar project required that he spend a month in Seattle, Washington, so Armstrong took his family along with him. During their trip to Seattle, little Karen fell and bumped her head while playing in a park. Later that day she seemed to have trouble focusing her eyes, and her parents, fearing she might have a concussion, took her to a doctor. Upon examining the child, the doctor found no signs of such an injury, but he urged the Armstrongs to have Karen examined by their regular physician when they returned home. The symptoms continued, and Karen's condition grew progressively worse. Finally, more extensive testing revealed a brain tumor. Armstrong was torn. He wanted to be with his family, but he had to continue his work on the X-15, which required him to make regular visits to the contractor's headquarters in Minneapolis, Minnesota. As a compromise, Armstrong divided his time between Minneapolis, working on the control system design, and Los Angeles, California, where the rest of the family stayed while Karen underwent radiation treatments to shrink the tumor. Although treatment brought about a brief period of remission, Karen died on January 28, 1962, shortly after her third birthday.

Armstrong was grief-stricken, but he had work to do. On April 20 of the same year, Armstrong, piloting the X-15 rocket

Armstrong poses with the X-15 rocket plane after a flight.

plane, reached an altitude of 207,500 feet and a speed of 3,989 miles per hour. Despite this achievement, Armstrong was rethinking his commitment to the X-15 program.

Two months earlier John Glenn had actually piloted *Friendship 7* through two of its three orbits, which suggested that astronauts need not be helpless passengers on spaceflights. "Dyno-Soar was still earthbound and I began to realize that the Gemini-Apollo programs were going to take man far beyond the mere fringes of the atmosphere and into deep space. Since it was in my real interest, I'd better get aboard,"[31] Armstrong recalled. So, in the spring of 1962, when NASA announced that it was accepting applications for a second astronaut training group, Armstrong applied.

Astronaut Training

Armstrong was one of 253 astronaut applicants considered by NASA during the spring of 1962. In June of that year, Armstrong became one of nine men chosen to be in the second astronaut group.

The months following his acceptance into the training program were busy ones for the Armstrong family. They moved to Houston, Texas; Armstrong began his astronaut training; and a second son, Mark, was born in April 1963.

While the family of four was temporarily crammed into an apartment, the Armstrongs helped design their new home, which was built in El Lago, twenty miles south of the city near the Manned Spacecraft Center. But bad luck had followed the family. Shortly after the Armstrongs moved into their new home, the house burned to the ground, destroying most of the family's belongings, including Armstrong's collection of model airplanes. The family escaped uninjured, and they later rebuilt their home on the same lot. Armstrong, however, had little time to enjoy it; he had to start training for his assignment as part of the backup crew of *Gemini 5*.

Eventually, Armstrong made it into space, aboard *Gemini 8*. The Gemini program was designed to gather the knowledge and develop the skills that Moon missions would later demand, such as docking with another spacecraft in Earth's orbit. Armstrong and astronaut David Scott lifted off on March 16, 1966, at 11:41 A.M. At 6:15 P.M. they successfully docked with an Agena satellite.

It was during *Gemini 8* that NASA experienced its first emergency in space. About thirty minutes after docking, the joined crafts began to roll. To prevent damage to both the space capsule and the satellite, the two craft separated. But after undocking from Agena, *Gemini 8* began rolling even faster. The roll, which occurred because one

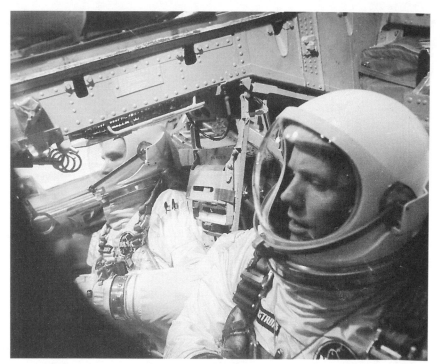

Pilot David Scott (left) and command pilot Neil Armstrong (right) inspect the Gemini 8 *spacecraft during flight simulations.*

of *Gemini*'s thruster rockets had failed to turn off, was dangerous since it could have caused the crew to lose consciousness. Armstrong had to fire one of the reentry thrusters in the opposite direction to stop the rolling and stabilize the craft. Now short of fuel, *Gemini 8* had to abort the rest of its mission. Flight controllers worked frantically to bring the craft back to Earth in an area where there was still enough daylight for a rescue team to spot them.

Gemini 8 splashed down in the northern Pacific Ocean and was spotted by aircraft half an hour later. A rescue team parachuted into the ocean and attached a flotation collar to keep the craft afloat until a ship could retrieve it. The astronauts and their three-man rescue team bobbed in the ocean for three hours before being picked up by the ship *Leonard F. Mason*. Following their return, Armstrong and Scott were presented with NASA's Exceptional Service Medal for the resourcefulness and courage they had shown in the face of a real space emergency.

Apollo 11

Armstrong's first spaceflight marked the end of the Gemini program and the transition to the next phase, Apollo. But a fire in their capsule killed the three astronauts assigned to *Apollo 1*, and it was nearly two years before another American flew in space.

All of the astronauts knew that a Moon landing was the goal of the Apollo project, but no one knew which mission would make the actual landing. It was not until January 6, 1969, that NASA informed Armstrong that he would be the commander of *Apollo 11*, and that his was the mission that would attempt the first lunar landing. Joining Armstrong would be Michael Collins and Buzz Aldrin. Over the next five months, the three men trained for ten to twelve hours per day, six days a week.

Finally, the day for the launch was at hand. On July 16 at 7:32 A.M., *Apollo 11* lifted off the ground. Jan Armstrong was well aware of the dangers her husband and the other astronauts faced. "Neil used to come home with his face drawn white, and I was worried about him. I was worried about all of them,"[32] she recalled.

Spectators watch and take pictures as Apollo 11 *lifts off on July 16, 1969, embarking on the first manned mission to land on the Moon.*

Once their craft had broken free of Earth's gravity, the crew settled into their routine housekeeping chores for the journey to the Moon. The three men exulted in the trip. They especially enjoyed the weightless environment. Aldrin put it into words: "I'll tell you, I've been having a ball floating around inside here, back and forth, up to one place and back to another."[33]

By the morning of the fourth day, the astronauts had a fantastic sight outside their window. Armstrong remarked, "The view of the moon we've been having recently is really spectacular. It fills about three-quarters of the hatch window. . . . It's a view worth the price of the trip."[34]

Soon, it was time to attempt what President John F. Kennedy had proposed years earlier. As *Apollo 11* was orbiting the moon, the command module, known as *Columbia*, the part of the craft that would remain in lunar orbit, undocked from the landing module, which had been named *Eagle*. Collins would stay aboard

A photo taken by Armstrong (who is reflected in Aldrin's helmet) on July 21, 1969, shows Buzz Aldrin on the Moon.

the command module, and Armstrong and Aldrin would continue the journey to the Moon's surface. *Eagle* began its descent in nose-down position. Armstrong turned the craft around as the descent continued: 2,000 feet, 750 feet, 400 feet, 330 feet. Large rocks loomed in the planned landing site, so Armstrong diverted to a clearer spot nearby. The technicians at the command center back on Earth held their breath as Armstrong made necessary corrections. Finally, *Eagle* was on the Moon's surface and shouts of joy erupted from the control room.

Once down, Armstrong and Aldrin began lengthy preparations for exiting *Eagle*. They climbed into the bulky suits and the backpacks that would be their portable living environment, and then they depressurized the cabin. Just over 109 hours into the mission, on July 20, Armstrong descended the ladder. A few moments later came these words from the Moon: "That's one small step for a man, one giant leap for mankind."[35]

A few moments later, Armstrong was joined by Aldrin. Once on the Moon's surface, Armstrong and Aldrin set about collecting rock, soil, and core samples. "There were a lot of things to do," Armstrong recalled, "and we had a hard time getting finished. . . . The primary difficulty was just far too little time to do the variety of things we would have liked. We had the problem of the five-year-old boy in the candy store."[36]

In addition to collecting samples and maneuvering in the Moon's much lower gravity, the astronauts set up instruments that were intended to continue sending information, such as seismic data, back to Earth after the astronauts departed the Moon.

Before returning to their craft, the astronauts unveiled a plaque attached to the base of the landing module, which would be left on the Moon's surface when they blasted off to return to the command module. The inscription read, "Here Men from the planet Earth first set foot upon the Moon, July 1969 A.D. We came in peace for all mankind."[37]

After two-and-a-half hours, Armstrong and Aldrin returned to the landing module with their rock samples. They carefully stowed and secured all of their samples in the cabin. Next, they reestablished the atmosphere inside the cabin and removed their bulky suits. Now they settled down to rest so they would be as alert as possible for the tricky job of redocking with the command module. But sleep was nearly impossible as Armstrong and Aldrin recalled their experiences on the Moon's surface and rehearsed in their minds all of the maneuvers that would be necessary for the life-or-death task of linking up with *Columbia*.

Eagle departed the Moon's surface a little less than twenty-two hours after it had landed. *Columbia* and *Eagle* maneuvered into position and successfully docked, and, for the first time on this flight, the astronauts could relax and enjoy the ride.

Some sixty hours later, Armstrong, Aldrin, and Collins splashed down in the Pacific Ocean on July 24, and were immediately whisked into quarantine. While scientists were reasonably certain there were no life-forms on the Moon, they were taking no risks with the possibility of infecting Earth with unknown bacteria. The astronauts were placed in an isolation van on the deck of the naval aircraft carrier *Hornet* and transported to Pearl Harbor, Hawaii, where the astronauts, still in their van, were airlifted to Hickam Air Force Base on Oahu and then loaded aboard an air force C-141 cargo plane for the flight to Houston.

After *Apollo 11*

The astronauts remained in quarantine for three weeks, and then it was time to face the world. As was traditional for returning heroes, New York City gave the three a tickertape parade. Among the honors that Armstrong received were NASA's Distinguished

President Richard Nixon visits the Apollo 11 *astronauts in quarantine, where they remained for three weeks after returning to Earth.*

Service Medal, the Congressional Space Medal of Honor, and the Medal of Freedom, the highest award presented to a U.S. civilian. Once the excitement subsided, Armstrong was ready for a quieter life. He went to work at NASA headquarters in Washington, D.C., coordinating all research and technology related to aeronautics. Within a couple of years, however, he resigned from NASA in 1971 and joined the faculty of the University of Cincinnati as a professor of aerospace engineering, a position he held for most of the seventies. Eventually, Armstrong moved on to the corporate world, first as chairman for computer technology for Aviation, Inc., and then as chairman of the board of A. I. L. Systems, Inc., an electronic systems company.

But as Armstrong enjoyed professional success, his home life deteriorated. In 1994, after a marriage of thirty-eight years, Neil and Jan Armstrong divorced. Neither has spoken publicly about the reasons for their divorce, and their friends and neighbors protect their privacy.

Neil Armstrong remains an intensely private individual. Armstrong so purposely avoids public attention that he even declined to attend most of the celebrations of the twenty-fifth anniversary of the lunar landing, held in July 1994. Some people were disappointed, even angered, by his decision. As one Wapakoneta resident observed, "Your hometown puts on a big festival celebrating the 25-year anniversary of something you did, the least you could do is show up!"[38]

Such remarks are, perhaps, an acknowledgment that feats like Armstrong's are larger than an individual, and that they do in a sense belong to all humankind.

CHAPTER 5

Sally Ride: Breaking the Barriers

When the space shuttle *Challenger* blasted into orbit on June 18, 1983, it carried a thirty-two-year-old physicist. That in itself was not a remarkable event; many scientists had already flown in space missions. What made this flight different was that this physicist was Sally Ride, the first American woman to travel in space.

A Childhood of Exploration and Discovery

Sally Kristin Ride was born on May 26, 1951, in Encino, California. Her father, Dale, was a professor of political science at what is today

Sally Ride, the first American woman in space.

Santa Monica College and her mother, Joyce, was a volunteer counselor at a women's prison. The Rides also had another daughter, Karen, nicknamed "Bear," who was born after Sally.

The atmosphere around the Ride household was nurturing and supportive. Sally and Karen were encouraged to be inquisitive and to develop both their intellectual and physical skills. Although they were never told that they had to *be* the best at anything, they were expected to always *do* their best at whatever they attempted.

It was soon obvious that Sally was a gifted individual. She could read the newspaper by the time she was five years old. As she grew older, her taste in reading evidenced an adventurous spirit: Nancy

Drew mysteries, Ian Flemming's James Bond books, and Superman comics all absorbed her. Sally did not spend all of her spare time reading, though; she was also interested in sports, especially tennis and softball.

When Sally was nine, her father took a year's leave from his teaching post and the family spent that year traveling throughout Europe. Sally and Karen's parents felt that this would be an excellent way to broaden the girls' cultural experiences. During this period Sally and Karen did not attend a formal school but were instead tutored by their parents. Since both parents had a background in education and both girls were good students with bright, inquisitive, disciplined minds, the Rides felt that home tutoring would serve to keep them abreast of their studies. The family visited many cultural and historical sites, and the girls spent a great deal of time in the company of people from a variety of cultures. The Rides' tutoring strategies proved successful; when Sally and Karen returned to school in California, they were so far ahead of other students their ages that they were both allowed to skip a grade.

About the time the Rides returned to the United States, Sally showed enough talent in tennis that her parents paid

Ride took tennis lessons from women's tennis champion Alice Marble (pictured).

for lessons with four-time women's national champion Alice Marble. By the time she was twelve, Sally was the eighteenth-ranked junior tennis player in the United States.

Sally's good grades and her skills on the tennis court earned her a scholarship at the exclusive Westlake School for Girls in Los Angeles. Most afternoons after her classes, she spent hours working on her game, often practicing with her school's headmaster, who soon found that Sally could be a fierce opponent. Later, he recalled one example of Ride's intensely competitive spirit. It was during a doubles match one afternoon when he fired a shot past her head. "She looked at me, smiled rather malevolently, and then fired . . . three successive drives aimed right between the eyes."[39]

It was, however, during her time at Westlake that Sally developed the serious interest in science, particularly physics, that would be her passion. For Sally, solving science problems appealed to her keen and orderly mind.

Although Sally was passionate about science and good at schoolwork, she was often bored in the classroom. She would watch the minutes tick slowly by on the clock, often daydreaming. Sally's teachers reported this behavior to her parents, but her parents chose not to pressure their daughter, only to insist that she keep up with her schoolwork.

In spite of her daydreaming, in 1969 Ride graduated from Westlake sixth in her class. She entered Swarthmore College in Swarthmore, Pennsylvania, in the fall of 1969, where she majored in physics. At Swarthmore, Ride continued playing tennis, winning the Eastern Intercollegiate Women's Tennis Championship two years in a row. Many people recognized Ride's talent on the tennis court. Some even encouraged her to consider dropping out of college to play professionally.

Although she declined to take up professional tennis, the sport did affect her life in other ways. Because Swarthmore had no indoor tennis courts and the campus and courts were often blanketed with snow during the winter months, Ride left Swarthmore for the warmer climate of the West Coast. Stanford University in Palo Alto, California, had an excellent physics department, and Ride transferred there. While at Stanford, she also developed an interest in literature, especially Shakespeare. It was a change of pace from her usual academic pursuits, "a break from the equations,"[40] as Ride described it. In fact, Ride graduated with a double major in physics and English literature.

For a time, Ride had considered pursuing English literature in graduate school, but physics won out. She first earned a master's degree, and then she went on to earn a Ph.D. in astrophysics.

It was while working on her doctorate in astrophysics that Ride read in the campus newspaper that NASA was searching for new astronaut candidates. Although the astronaut program had been an all-male domain, this time women were being encouraged to apply. She submitted her application, and of the 8,000 applicants, Ride became one of the 208 finalists.

All of the finalists were subjected to an extensive testing process, both physically and mentally. One part of the testing process was two forty-five minute interviews with teams of psychiatrists. The interviews were handled along a "good guy, bad guy" format, with the "bad guy" trying to shake the candidate's composure. Not a person to be easily rattled, Ride made good scores in these interviews. When the final decision was made, Ride was one of thirty-five selected, six of whom were women.

Ride Makes the Team

Sally Ride reported to NASA for duty in July 1978. Along with the other trainees, Ride underwent an intensive year-long training program that included parachute jumping, water survival, riding a huge centrifuge to get the feeling of positive G forces at take off, radio communication, and navigation. To accustom themselves to weightlessness the new astronauts took training flights in the KC-135, nicknamed "the Vomit Comet" because so many passengers suffered nausea during the alternating climbs and dives that simulated the weightless conditions of space.

Since each astronaut had to be able to fill any role aboard the shuttle, Ride had to learn how to actually pilot the craft. To prepare for this eventuality, she took flying lessons. She enjoyed flying so much that she earned her pilot's license and flying became a favorite hobby.

During the year's packed training schedule, Ride and her fellow astronauts were expected to learn about the operations of the basic shuttle systems. Additionally, each astronaut was required to become an expert in at least one function of the shuttle.

Physical training was rigorous as well. In addition to the parachute jumps over both land and water and survival training, Ride and her

The "Vomit Comet" made steep climbs (left) and dives to give trainees the experience of weightlessness (right).

Ride learned to fly as part of her training and enjoyed it so much that she went on to earn a pilot's license.

fellow trainees ran four miles each weekday, eight to ten miles per day on the weekends; to build strength, all worked out with weights.

In the summer of 1979, Ride and her classmates completed their astronaut training, and their names were put on the list for future shuttle flights. In the meantime, there was plenty of work to do on Earth. One of Ride's assignments as she awaited her opportunity to fly in space was working on the team that designed a remote control mechanical arm to be used in deploying and retrieving space satellites. The fifty-foot robotic arm would travel into space in the shuttle's cargo bay and would be used to deploy and retrieve scientific equipment as well as satellites.

Although most of the trainees' waking hours were devoted to training that first year in the astronaut program, Ride managed to have some social life. Among the other astronauts, one in particular, Steven Hawley, interested her. Despite their busy schedules, Ride and Hawley continued dating one another, and, in July 1982, they were married. Since this was the first wedding between two American astronauts and promised to become a major media event, they kept the news of their wedding secret from all but their closest friends and family. Ride and Hawley were married in a small, informal ceremony in the groom's parents' backyard. Some aspects of the wedding were out of the ordinary. For one thing, the bride-to-be piloted herself to the ceremony, flying a jet from Houston to Kansas. The bride and groom, both informally clad in blue jeans, were united in marriage by two ministers: the groom's father, the Reverend Bernard Hawley, and the bride's sister, the Reverend Karen Scott.

The honeymoon was brief because work waited for the two astronauts back at NASA and an especially important assignment awaited Sally Ride. The assignment that Ride had been given was to serve in the critical role of capcom, or capsule communicator. The capcom is the one person at Mission Control who is allowed to speak with the astronauts in space. The capcom passes along information to the astronauts from the scientists, technicians, and other ground support crew, and he or she relays information from the astronauts to ground control. Sally Ride was the first woman capcom in the history of NASA, and she served in this capacity during the second and third flights of the space shuttle *Columbia* in November 1981 and March 1982.

The Flight of Mission STS-7

Finally, one job remained for Sally Ride, the job for which she had spent the past five years of her life preparing: her mission in space. Ride was assigned to Mission STS-7, as the *Challenger*'s flight was formally designated. In addition to being the first woman in space, she would also be the youngest American astronaut to fly a mission. Additionally, at this time Ride was the only space-bound astronaut who was married to another astronaut.

Aboard *Challenger* would be mission specialist John Fabian, pilot Frederick Hauck, commander Robert L. Crippin, mission specialist Sally Ride, and Norman Thagard. Thagard was a medical doctor who was added to the crew to study the motion sickness that had plagued so many astronauts. The addition of Thagard to the crew brought the total number on board to five, the largest space shuttle ever at that time. On June 18, 1983, *Challenger* lifted into space carrying America's first woman astronaut.

As mission specialist, Ride's duties focused mainly on the operation of the remote manipulator system (RMS), the fifty-foot-long remote control robotic arm that she had helped design. Ride and Fabian used the robotic arm to deploy four satellites, including *Anik-C*, a Canadian communications satellite, and *Palpa B*, an Indonesian communications satellite that would provide telephone service to a million people in Southeast Asia. Ride and Fabian also used the arm to deploy and retrieve an experiment platform that orbited alongside the shuttle for part of the mission.

Ride's spirits during the mission were exceptionally high, and she was usually in the middle of the pranks and games played aboard the shuttle. One impromptu game involved a jar of jelly beans. The astronauts released the jelly beans in the weightless environment of the shuttle and then darted about, bouncing off the bulkheads and catching the jelly beans in their mouths. "The thing I most remember about the flight is that it was fun," Ride recalled later. "In fact, I'm sure it's the most fun I'll ever have in my life."[41]

Upon *Challenger*'s return to Earth, Ride, the first astronaut down the steps of the shuttle, faced a barrage of questions from reporters. In the wake of her first flight, she had offers of television programs, interviews, and movies about her life. Ride was neither impressed nor interested in any of the offers. "I didn't go into the space program to make money or be famous," she said. Ride's intentions were the same as they had been when she entered the space program: "I didn't enter this program to be the first [American] woman in space. I came to get a chance to fly in space."[42]

Sally Rides Again

Although Mission STS-7 was the trip for which she gained the most attention, it was not her only journey into space. Ride's next mission was aboard NASA's one hundredth spaceflight and the thirteenth shuttle flight, STS-41G. Once again she was aboard *Challenger*, which lifted off from Cape Canaveral, Florida, on October 5, 1984, and again Ride would be part of the largest shuttle team to date. The mission did not receive the same degree of media attention, although a number of "firsts" were part of the flight. This was the first shuttle team to include two women, Ride and Dr. Kathryn Sullivan.

Sullivan became the first American woman to make a space walk; and Ride became the first mission specialist to make a second shuttle flight.

The space shuttle's remote manipulator system launches a satellite. Ride had helped design the RMS and operated the robotic arm during her space flight.

Technical glitches plagued the flight, but Ride was instrumental in overcoming at least one of them. One of the crew's assignments was to deploy a weather satellite. The satellite had two solar panels, which had been folded closed in order to save room in the cargo bay. However, when Ride prepared to deploy the satellite, the solar panels were frozen in the closed position. This type of problem had not been foreseen in any training drill, so Ride had to employ her problem-solving skills to improvise a solution. First, she used the robotic arm to turn the weather satellite in the bay and position it so that the Sun's rays could thaw the panels. Once the panels had been warmed, Ride used the robotic arm to jiggle the satellite, which shook the panels open. Finally, three hours behind schedule, the weather satellite

Ride's resourcefulness helped the crew overcome the technical difficulties that hampered the STS-41G mission.

was successfully deployed. Despite problems, the mission came to a successful conclusion, landing at Cape Canaveral on October 13. By the end of Mission STS-41G, Ride had accumulated 343 hours in space.

As Ride prepared for her third space mission, the worst accident in the history of American space flight occurred, the explosion of *Challenger* on January 28, 1986. The *Challenger* disaster, with the loss of the entire crew of seven, brought a temporary halt to the space shuttle program. President Ronald Reagan appointed a special commission to assess the causes of the accident, and Ride was the only active astronaut selected to serve on this commission.

The investigation concluded that the lines of communication among NASA's many departments was faulty. It also concluded that there had been many engineering flaws and human errors and that safety margins built into flight procedures were inadequate. In cutting too many corners, the panal concluded, NASA had not allowed enough down time between missions to allow for the safety of the craft and the astronauts. Finally, the commission recommended that astronauts and engineers should have a greater role in approving or scrubbing future launches.

But despite the changes that NASA would implement for future missions, morale was already seriously damaged; a number of qualified, experienced astronauts left the shuttle program. Among those departing was Sally Ride. Normally not outspoken, Ride stated in an interview that space travel was still a risky operation. "I am not ready to fly again. I think there are very few astronauts who are ready to fly again now. I think we may have been misleading people into thinking that this is a routine operation, that it's just like getting on an airliner and going across the country and that it's safe. And it's not."[43]

Exit NASA, Enter Teaching

Following the completion of the *Challenger* inquiry, Ride stayed on at NASA until she had completed an assessment of the country's future in space exploration. Among the recommendations Ride made was that a base be established on the Moon, large enough to accomodate as many as thirty people at a time. She also encouraged the use of robotics in space exploration.

Feeling that she had completed her work there, Ride left NASA in August 1987 to join the faculty of her alma mater, Stanford University. "She was very enthusiastic about coming back here and getting involved in an academic environment," said Stanford spokesman Bob Beyers in announcing her appointment. "Dr. Ride will be free to select her own topic of study as well as the place she needs to conduct her research,"[44] he said.

For the next two years, Ride worked at Stanford's Center for International Security and Arms Control, training scientists in procedures relating to arms control and national security.

Ride's stay at Stanford was relatively brief, and in 1989 she moved to San Diego, where she was appointed director of the California Space Institute, which is associated with the University of California at San Diego. There, she resumed her study of free-electron lasers in addition to coordinating space research among the university's eight campuses around the state. Another of her duties was to work with California companies developing products for use in space.

Throughout the 1990s, Ride took an active role in improving science education in American public schools, and she continues to do so. As part of this effort, Ride and a colleague, JoBea Way, established a three-year project that involved students in the space shuttle program firsthand. Under this program, which was known as KidSat: Mission Operations, students had the opportunity to plan real research projects for shuttle missions. Among the projects participated in by both high school and college students have been the examination of Earth's biomes, weather patterns, and the

Sally Ride's accomplishments have earned her awards as well as public admiration. Here, Ride gives an autograph after her first spaceflight.

flow of rivers on Earth's surface. Other projects were designed to reach younger students. For example, Ride has written two children's books: *To Space and Back, Voyager: An Adventure to the Edge of the Solar System,* and *The Third Planet: Exploring the Earth from Space.*

Always on the lookout for new opportunities to develop public support for space exploration, in June 1999 Ride joined the board of directors of a company known as space.com. Space.com has the only site on the Internet that is devoted to news, information, education, and entertainment focused on space and space-related content. "Sally will be involved in every area of space.com, bringing her vast knowledge and depth of understanding to all aspects of our enterprise," the company's chief executive, Lou Dobbs, said. "We're delighted that she has joined our team and know that she will be making significant contributions to space.com."[45]

At the opening of the twenty-first century, Ride maintains a busy speaking schedule, traveling throughout the world. Ride's work has won her many awards and honors, but her place in history will remain clearly defined as the first American woman to fly in space. The far-reaching effects of her accomplishment were best summed up by women's rights activist Gloria Steinem when she commented following Ride's first shuttle flight, "It's an important first, because it means millions and millions of little girls are going to sit in front of the television and know they can become astronauts after this."[46]

CHAPTER 6

Christa McAuliffe: The Teacher and the Dream

Christa McAuliffe is best remembered as the teacher in space, the "ordinary citizen" who lost her life in the greatest disaster in the history of the American space program. But to those who knew her best, Christa McAuliffe is remembered as a thoughtful daughter, a caring sister, a loving wife and mother, and an exceptional educator.

A Freewheeling Spirit

Christa McAuliffe was born in the Boston suburb of Framingham, Massachusetts, on September 2, 1948, the first of five children born to Edward and Grace Corrigan. Her early life did not seem promising, for as a baby, Christa suffered from several illnesses. The most serious of these were upper respiratory problems and digestive disorders, which sent her back to the hospital on several occasions. So severe were these problems that there were times when her parents feared that their daughter would not live to see her first birthday. Her mother recalled one particularly severe case of asthmatic bronchitis: "We worried about going to sleep. We were scared to death she wouldn't be breathing when we woke up."[47]

Although she was frail, Christa proved to be an unusually bright child. According to her parents, she never used baby talk and spoke in complete sentences from an early age. She could recite nursery rhymes by the time she was eighteen months old, but, since Christa was their first child, the Corrigans did not realize that this was exceptional behavior for a child so young.

Aside from being gifted, Christa was also virtually fearless, which got her into plenty of trouble. Once when she was a toddler, Christa was caught pedaling her tricycle down the middle of a busy Framingham street. She was saved from certain injury or death by a neighbor, who brought her back to the safety of the sidewalk. She gained such a reputation for mischief that her parents had difficulty finding a baby-sitter when they needed one.

As time went on, the Corrigan family grew, and Christa had to share her parents' attention first with a brother, Christopher; then another brother, Steven; and finally two sisters, Betsy and the last of the Corrigan kids, Lisa, who arrived when Christa was ten years old. Christa was a loving and supportive big sister, and when she was older, she often baby-sat for her siblings.

When not helping out at home with her little brothers and sisters, Christa was involved in team sports, such as basketball and softball, and in scouting activities. Often, Christa was the one her teammates looked to for leadership. "She always took over any situation and acted older than her age,"[48] recalled her mother.

Christa also showed a talent in music. To develop that talent, she took dance, voice, and piano lessons. Her father encouraged

From an early age, Christa McAuliffe showed the courage and intellect that would help her become the first "ordinary citizen" chosen to go into space.

her singing and would provide piano accompaniment. Often, he would invite neighbors to share an evening of music. Convinced that his daughter had real ability, Corrigan encouraged her to enter community talent shows.

As Christa entered her teen years, she remained close to her parents, often bending her talents to create gifts for them. For example, when she was fifteen, she made her father a ceramic manger scene for Christmas, and the next year she made a long velvet and lace dress for her mother. Mrs. Corrigan wore the dress during the Christmas season for many years after that.

School Days

Although her parents never pressured her to do well in school, Christa pushed herself—perhaps too hard at times. When her second grade teacher noticed that Christa was struggling and frustrated with writing practice, the teacher spoke with Christa's parents. "Christa has to accept the fact that she can't do everything perfectly. I'm afraid she'll be disappointed if she spends the rest of her life as a perfectionist."[49]

Christa's drive for perfection served her well when, in 1961, she entered Marion High School. Marion was a small Catholic secondary school with the reputation of being strong in academics and strict on discipline. The nuns wore traditional long black habits with white bibs; the students were required to wear uniforms.

Christa's interest in sports and music carried over into high school. In 1964 Christa was pitcher for the girl's parish softball team, which won a local championship. She also found time to sing in school musicals, such as a performance of the Rogers and Hammerstein play *The Sound of Music*. In addition to sports and music, Christa held down a variety of part-time jobs. With such a crowded schedule, something had to suffer. Often Christa would arrive late to her classes, much to the displeasure of the nuns at Marion High, and her tardiness earned her punishment in the form of detention.

In typical fashion, the first day of her sophomore year, Christa arrived late to her homeroom class. Watching from the back of the classroom was a new transfer student named Steven James McAuliffe. The attraction the two felt for one another was strong and almost immediate. From the first day he met Christa, Steve never had eyes for anyone else, and Christa had similar loyalty for Steve. As Christa later told her parents, she would date Steve or she would rather not date at all.

Christa enjoyed playing softball and was a pitcher for her parish's softball team in high school.

But despite her feelings for Steve, the focus of her life lay elsewhere, for Christa was obsessed with helping those less fortunate than herself. She helped start a food basket program at her school for needy families, and she worked on charity committees and programs through her church and girl scout troop.

"I never felt good about myself if I wasn't giving," she recalled years later. "I felt like I was cheating myself and everyone else I had a chance to help."[50]

As part of her commitment to helping others, Christa decided that she wanted to become a teacher, so following her graduation from high school, Christa enrolled at Framingham State College, majoring in education. Framingham State had the advantage of being close by, which meant that money that would have otherwise been spent on room and board was available to pay for her siblings' college educations as well.

Throughout her college years, Christa's relationship with her father remained close. When Steve, now her fiancé, could not be in town for Framingham's senior's dance, she asked her father to take her, "because I have enough respect for myself that I won't feel uncomfortable going with my father,"[51] she said at the time.

While Christa attended Framingham State, Steve McAuliffe went off to the Virginia Military Institute. The two remained loyal to one another, though, and finally, after a four-year, long-distance engagement, and seven years after their first meeting, Christa and Steve married.

Taking on a Tough Job

Right after their wedding, twenty-one-year-old Christa and Steve loaded their old Volkswagen and a rented trailer with everything they owned, including their wedding gifts, and moved to Washington, D.C. The young couple settled into a tiny apartment with a leaky roof. Neither of the newlyweds had a job. Steve had been admitted to Georgetown University's law school, and Christa was looking for teaching positions. Openings for teachers were scarce, but just a week before school began, Christa found a job as a full-time substitute teacher at Benjamin Foulois Junior High School in nearby Morningside, Maryland.

McAuliffe with some of her students in 1985. McAuliffe's first teaching job was as a full-time substitute at a junior high school near Washington, D.C.

Working as a substitute was trying, even for an upbeat person like Christa McAuliffe. After she had been teaching a few months, she wrote to her mother, telling of her frustrations: "The kids at school have calmed down, but there are still a few I'd like to string up. My seventh period class is a zoo. I found out through the faculty lounge that I have the largest class load in the school outside of the gym instructors—great!"[52]

McAuliffe's first full-time teaching job was also a difficult assignment. Thomas Johnson Junior High was an inner city school in Lanham, Maryland, with a tough reputation, a different sort of environment for a young woman who had spent most of her life in a white, middle-class suburb. It took a while for McAuliffe to be accepted by both her colleagues and her students. Christa McAuliffe's enthusiasm and willingness to work with the most problematic students soon won over the other teachers. Playing games with her classes, such as Dangerous Parallel, a foreign policy–simulation game, and her one-on-one attention for her charges won over the students. She fought for field trips for her social studies students so they could see some of the places they read about in their textbooks. One trip was an all-day field trip to the Civil War battlefield at Gettysburg, Pennsylvania. Another trip took them to the FBI Building in Washington. Always, the goal was to expand her students' horizons.

Through hard work, the McAuliffe family prospered. It also began to grow. On September 11, 1976, the McAuliffes welcomed their first child, Scott Corrigan McAuliffe. Three years later, on August 24, 1979, Scott was joined by a sister, Caroline.

It was during the months before Caroline's birth that McAuliffe began keeping a written journal. McAuliffe's own writing sparked her interest in the journals of early pioneer women. In hopes of nurturing a similar interest among her students, she introduced journal keeping into the social studies curriculum at Concord High School, the school where she now taught.

It appeared that McAuliffe's life had settled into a predictable balance of teaching, parenthood, and volunteer work. But in August 1984, shortly before the beginning of the new school year, Christa and Steve heard an announcement on the car radio that would make history.

The president was making a speech in which he was emphasizing his administration's commitment to education. "Today,"

In 1984 President Ronald Reagan announced that a teacher would be selected to travel into space.

President Reagan said, "I am directing NASA to begin a search in all of our elementary and secondary schools, and to choose as the first passenger in the history of our space program one of America's finest: a teacher."[53]

Everyone who knew her, including her husband, encouraged McAuliffe to apply, but with so many home and job responsibilities, she kept putting off sending in her application. She almost waited too long. The application was lengthy and required a great deal of thought.

One question on the application asked her opinion of why it was important for a teacher to fly in space. McAuliffe answered, "Space is the future. If as teachers we don't prepare the students for the future, we're not doing our jobs. We have to include it." She also went on to say that people should "see space as a frontier . . . to show there is a new way of living."[54]

McAuliffe was one of 11,500 applicants. Some campaigns conducted by the would-be teacher-astronauts were attention-grabbing and sometimes silly, like two teachers who passed out campaign buttons like politicians in a bid for media attention. During the review of applications, the pool of 11,500 candidates was eventually narrowed to an elite group of ten finalists. And one of those finalists was Christa McAuliffe.

McAuliffe did not consider her chances of being selected for the flight to be very high. Most of the finalists had proposed sophisticated and complicated projects in their applications. Several involved complicated scientific experiments, such as a study of the reproductive system of flies in zero gravity. McAuliffe's proposed project was to keep a simple journal, a record of her adventures as a space pioneer in the same way women over a hundred years earlier had kept journals of their frontier experiences. McAuliffe stated, "I want to humanize the space age by giving the perspective of a nonastronaut. I think the students will look at that and see that an ordinary person is contributing to history. If they can make that connection, they are going to get excited about history and about the future."[55]

She felt that, due to the simplicity of her idea, her project might not be considered as seriously as those of the other candidates. She also felt somewhat intimidated by some of the candidates. One had been a union activist, another a computer program designer, and a third was a former air force pilot. McAuliffe did not think that her professional background would compare very favorably with these.

There was also a moment when she had a brief second thought about being the first teacher in space. Because astronauts must spend a lengthy amount of time away from their families as launch dates grow closer, McAuliffe paused briefly to consider exactly what the consequences might be if she were selected for the flight. Was she being fair to her husband and to her children? The cost to her family in terms of the lost privacy also worried her: Television and newspaper reporters would be literally camped out on the McAuliffes' doorstep. But McAuliffe knew she had the unwavering support of her family and her community. Moreover, she had never left a job unfinished.

McAuliffe forged ahead, enduring the rounds of medical and psychological tests that all ten finalists were subjected to. The weightlessness simulator, known as "the Vomit Comit," worried her, though, because she had suffered from motion sickness as a child.

At the conclusion of the evaluations, the ten finalists were flown to Washington, D.C., for a final round of interviews with seven of NASA's senior officials. Finally, the winner was announced.

The Teacher in Space

The ten finalists filed into the Roosevelt Room in the White House, where then vice president George Bush would make the announcement. First he announced that second grade teacher Barbara Morgan would be the alternate who would fly if the person selected, but as yet unknown to the public, was—for any reason—unable to make the trip. Then he made the announcement that the finalists, the press, and many Americans had been waiting for: "And the winner, the teacher who will be going into space, is Christa McAuliffe."[56] McAuliffe stepped to the microphone. Her remarks were brief and focused on the other candidates. "It is not often a teacher is at a loss for words. I know my students wouldn't think so. I've made nine wonderful friends over the last two weeks, and when that shuttle goes, there might be one body, but there's gonna be ten souls I'm takin' with me."[57]

As McAuliffe had expected, the news media assault began almost immediately. Reporters descended on Steve McAuliffe outside of his law office, television helicopters buzzed over the McAuliffe home in Concord, New Hampshire, and the phone rang constantly. Nine-year-old Scott, the McAuliffe's oldest child, was annoyed by the attention of the press and simply wanted his mother to come home.

After the announcement, McAuliffe returned to Concord to spend some time with her family. Although she wanted some private time with them, that was nearly impossible. There were parades, speeches, and ceremonies for McAuliffe and her family to attend; now a national celebrity, she had to travel several times to appear on television programs like *The Tonight Show*. Despite the commotion, the family did manage a brief vacation together on Cape Cod at a friend's cottage before McAuliffe flew to Houston early in September 1985 to begin the training that would culminate in the flight scheduled for January 1986.

A Teacher Becomes An Astronaut

Much of McAuliffe's training took place in a simulator, a mock-up of the space shuttle cockpit, which was controlled by a system of computers. In the shuttle simulator, the crew trained for all kinds of emergencies, from engine failure to flight control problems. And, to McAuliffe's dismay, there would also be more time in the Vomit Comet.

McAuliffe and her alternate, Barbara Morgan, also devoted a lot of time to preparing the plans for lessons that McAuliffe

McAuliffe hugs a fellow teacher after Vice President George Bush announced that she had been chosen to ride in the space shuttle.

would present from space. The plan was for Morgan to assist her from the ground by serving as a television commentator. McAuliffe was to present two live lessons from the shuttle and also to videotape a series of science demonstrations that would be distributed to schools throughout the country after the shuttle's return to Earth.

Although McAuliffe was giving her best and working as hard as the other six astronauts whom she would accompany into space, she sometimes felt inferior. For one thing, the other astronauts were in top physical condition, and although McAuliffe jogged and played volleyball, she felt she was not as fit as her fellow team members. She also knew that some people at NASA felt that her science background left a lot to be desired. This led to tension between McAuliffe and Bob Mayfield, a Texas science teacher who worked with NASA as educational coordinator.

Mayfield had trouble communicating with McAuliffe and blamed her. "This would be a lot easier if she knew science," he said midway through the training. "We don't speak the same vocabulary."[58] McAuliffe was strong-willed and resisted Mayfield's approach to presenting the science lessons. McAuliffe reasoned that NASA had decided to send a teacher into space, and it should therefore leave educational decisions to her. This was an argument McAuliffe won.

Homesickness was another big issue. She missed her family and friends. She missed things like reading to her children at bedtime, sitting in her favorite church pew, and teaching in her classroom. She even missed sharing household chores with her husband, Steve.

She made a brief visit home in October 1985, and her family was able to come see her for a few days in November. This helped make the long months away from home more bearable. Then, with most of their preparations complete, the shuttle crew was given a break for the Christmas holidays.

One of the first things that McAuliffe did when she got home was to visit her hair stylist for a haircut and a perm. She did not want her hair floating about and getting in her way in zero grav-

McAuliffe (left) and her alternate, Barbara Morgan (center), look over astronaut supplies during their training.

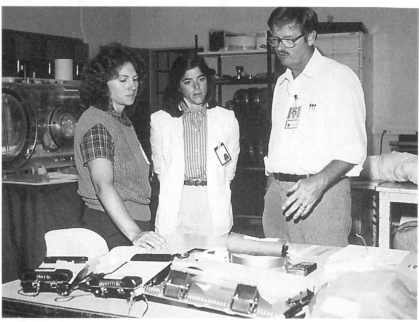

ity. There was much to do during this brief visit. Then, all too soon, it was time to return to Houston to finish preparing for the ultimate field trip.

Final Preparations and the Launch

The crew, including McAuliffe, was ready, but the shuttle *Columbia*, which was scheduled for a mission ahead of *Challenger*'s, was delayed seven times, which in turn delayed the *Challenger* mission. McAuliffe was impatient to be on her way, realizing that the delays in the launch schedule might push the *Challenger* launch date as far back as late February or even March. She had invited 350 guests to witness the launch, and the delays would play havoc with their plans. Still, she was pleased that NASA officials were cautious with the safety of the astronauts and the shuttles.

In January 1986 the *Challenger* crew flew to the Kennedy Space Center in Florida to begin a series of dress rehearsals in preparation for the launch that was still being pushed back. Over five days, the launch was postponed three times. The first delay was caused by the late return of the *Columbia* shuttle. The second launch date, January 23, was lost due to a dust storm at one of their alternate landing sites in Africa, and the scheduled January 26 launch was scrubbed due to rain showers. On Monday, January 27, it finally appeared that *Challenger* would get underway. The astronauts were on board, strapped into their seats two hours before the scheduled launch. Then, nine minutes before launch, a handle on a hatch stuck. Despite all of their expensive, high-tech equipment, technicians found that the battery was dead on the screwdriver they needed to fix the handle. In the time it took to locate a battery and repair the handle, the weather deteriorated and, once again, the launch was postponed. This was almost too much for the astronauts. This time, there were no waves or smiles when the crew members returned to their quarters.

In the predawn hours of Tuesday, January 28, the three-hour fuel loading procedure started all over again. The weather had cleared, but it had turned bitterly cold, by Florida standards at least. The windchill factor was ten degrees below zero, cold enough to disable some of the launch site cameras. Nevertheless, the astronauts and their support crew prepared for a launch. Before the astronauts boarded, technicians checked the shuttle and the support tower for ice. A crew member presented McAuliffe with an apple before she entered the craft. The temperature was twenty-seven degrees. One final ice check was made twenty minutes before launch time, and all appeared in order. Finally, after all of the delays, this one looked like a "go."

Automobiles pulled off to the side of the highway near the launch pad to watch the blast off. The drivers tuned their car radios. People lucky enough to have a view of the skies over the Kennedy Space Center watched from their offices and apartment windows.

The final countdown began at 11:29 A.M. The crowds overflowing the stands counted along. Ten, nine, eight, seven, six. . . . The main engines fired. . . . Five, four, three, two, one. . . . Ignition of the solid rocket boosters, then liftoff!

The crowd cheered as *Challenger* cleared the launch pad and accelerated toward the heavens. The capcom received the expected transmission from *Challenger*, "Go at throttle up."[59] Then, seventy-three seconds into the mission, a huge, sinister cloud erupted in the Florida skies and the crowds were stunned and silent. Eyewitnesses, Theresa Bruni and her husband, Ed, lived near the space center at that time. Over a dozen years later, she recalled the moment of the explosion:

> We were on the beach [Cocoa Beach] just past the air force base. It was freezing cold. I was taking pictures of it [the shuttle] going up. "Something's wrong with the shuttle!" I said to my husband. "It's not going up right. It's leaning, turning. I can't stand it. Something's wrong!" I handed my husband the camera. I couldn't look. To this day I can see it. I was horrendous, so horrendous. Even now I can't watch a launch. The smoke stayed in the sky so long. We cried. We cried all the way home.[60]

As the boosters spiraled off in different directions, their paths etched in the sky by smoking trails, debris from *Challenger* appeared to rain into the ocean in slow motion. In a billowing cloud, the Challenger mission ended.

After the Accident

As the country began recovering from the shock of the accident, NASA ordered an investigation. President Reagan also ordered a commission independent of NASA to examine all activities, procedures, and equipment involved in the launch. Former astronaut Neil Armstrong and active astronaut Sally Ride were among those appointed to serve on the commission. After months of study, the commission reported that the safety standards for the shuttle's

Seventy-three seconds after liftoff (left), Challenger *exploded (right), killing all seven on board.*

launch had been inadequate. They concluded that the tragedy probably could have been prevented. Sally Ride was so disturbed by the results that she decided she would not participate in another shuttle mission.

The commission also learned that engineers for Morton Thiokol, the company that manufactured the solid fuel booster rockets used on the shuttle, had issued a memo months before the accident, relaying its concerns that the O-rings used to seal the joints between the segments of the booster rockets might fail at low temperatures. The memo had detailed the way in which cold weather like that experienced the day of the launch could cause the O-rings to shrink and create what amounted to a huge blow torch pointed directly at the shuttle's main fuel tank.

In its final report, the commission made specific recommendations. The solid rocket boosters (SRBs) should be redesigned. In particular, it recommended that extra O-rings should be added to strengthen the joints between segments in the SRBs. Additionally, heaters should be installed to prevent shrinkage of the O-rings at low temperatures. Other proposed new safety procedures for the launches and landings were outlined, such as the inclusion of some sort of crew escape mechanism, taking more time for flight preparation, and greater safety margins for shuttle landings. Also, lines of communication between the departments at NASA would be restructured. All of these directives took time. It would be over a year and a half before another shuttle would fly.

Across the country, money was pledged to establish scholarships in Christa McAuliffe's and the rest of the *Challenger* crew's names. Dozens of school buildings around America were named in McAuliffe's honor, but her husband noted that these honors would be hollow if they were not accompanied by action: "If you sit on the sideline, reflect on Christa as a hero, or as a glorious representative or a canonized saint, rather than putting your energies into accomplishing for her what she wanted to do, then I think her efforts will have been in vain."[61]

McAuliffe accomplished one goal, however. In her thirty-seven years, Christa McAuliffe demonstrated to everyone that ordinary people are capable of extraordinary deeds.

CHAPTER 7

Mae Jemison: Exploring Space and Serving Humankind

On September 12, 1992, Dr. Mae Jemison stepped aboard the space shuttle *Endeavour*. A medical doctor and engineer, Jemison was making her first shuttle trip. She was also breaking a final barrier: When the *Endeavour* lifted off the launch pad, Jemison would be the first African American woman in space.

A Childhood of Discovery

Mae Carol Jemison was born on October 17, 1956, the youngest of three children. Her father, Charlie Jemison, was a carpenter, and her mother, Dorothy, was an elementary school teacher. Mae was born in Decator, Alabama, but since the family moved to Chicago when she was only three, she always considered Chicago as her hometown.

Dr. Mae Jemison, the first African American woman in space.

All three Jemison children were bright and curious, and the elder Jemisons sought to foster these qualities. When the children came to their parents with questions, instead of getting all of the information they requested, they were encouraged to seek out their own answers. Charlie and Dorothy Jemison felt that children learned better and retained more information when they had to locate the information for themselves. For example, when Mae was about seven years old, she got a splinter in her finger, which became infected. Mae wanted to know what the "white stuff" was that oozed from her finger. Her mother told her that it was called pus and convinced her daughter to read and see what she could find out about it. Mae became so involved in her investigation that she developed it into a school science project.

In addition to fostering curiosity, the Jemisons encouraged their children to set challenging goals for themselves, and Mae's goal was to be either a doctor or a scientist. By the time she was twelve, she already had a strong interest in science in general and space in particular. Mae's tastes in reading reflected those interests, as she liked to read both science fiction and books on astronomy.

In addition to reading, Mae also liked the television program *Star Trek*. One character on the show had a particular impact on Mae. The communications officer aboard the starship *Enterprise*, Lieutenant Uhura, played by African American actress Nichelle Nichols, was a strong African female holding an important position aboard the starship. As an adult, Jemison recalled in an interview that Nichols's character became her role model: "Right there on the screen, week in and week out, who could miss Lieutenant Uhura, the starship's stylish, self-assured communications officer—and a black woman, no less. . . . Images show us possibilities. A lot of times fantasy is what gets us through to reality."[63]

Although Mae was fascinated by science fiction, she was interested in problems that affected real people. While in high school, Mae decided to construct a science fair project on sickle cell anemia, a hereditary blood disease that attacks one in four hundred African Americans. Most of her research for the project was done at a local hospital. She enjoyed her experience in the hospital laboratory so much that, when she finished her project, she applied for and got a job in the lab.

Although she was an extremely bright student and could have focused solely on her studies, Mae had interests other than her classes. She was active in the modern dance club in her high school and was on the cheerleading squad. She was also interested in art and in archaeology. But even while participating in such a wide variety of activities, Mae was on a fast track and graduated from Morgan Park High School in 1973 at sixteen years of age.

The Fast Track Continues

Jemison had planned on attending college, and a National Achievement Scholarship helped make that possible. These scholarships are awarded to African American high school students who maintain high academic standards throughout their high school years. With her scholarship in hand, she chose to attend prestigious Stanford University in Palo Alto, California. There, she majored in both chemical engineering and Afro-American studies.

Although Stanford was a well-known university with top professors and a demanding curriculum, Jemison was not awed by the school's reputation. "I was naïve and stubborn enough that it didn't phase me," she later recalled. "It's not until recently that I realized

Star Trek's *Lieutenant Uhura was one of Jemison's role models.*

that sixteen was particularly young or that there were even any issues associated with my parents having enough confidence to [allow me to] go that far from home."[63]

In addition to engineering and Afro-American studies, she studied several foreign languages and became fluent in Swahili, Japanese, and Russian. Carrying a double major and studying languages would have been more than enough for most students, but to this already jam-packed schedule Jemison added an interest in student politics. She became the first female president of the Black Student Union. She also took part in college theater productions, producing plays and choreographing the dance routines for musicals.

Later, Jemison recalled her college years as being mostly a positive experience. There were some professors, however, who seemed to have a problem with having a young black woman in their classes; thus, Jemison felt that she was always expected to prove herself to be "worthy" to be studying for a degree in chemical engineering. She credits this experience with helping her to become stronger and more determined to achieve her goals.

In four years' time, despite all of her extra activities, she completed her degree requirements. In 1977, at twenty years of age, Jemison graduated with a bachelor of science degree in chemical

Jemison studied medicine at Cornell University (pictured), receiving her medical degree in 1981.

engineering and a bachelor of arts degree in Afro-American studies. Despite her many interests, Jemison retained her childhood goal of becoming a doctor, so she continued her education, pursuing a medical degree at Cornell University.

Jemison completed her training at Cornell in 1981 and was assigned to her medical internship at the University of Southern California Medical Center in Los Angeles.

Once she had completed her internship, Jemison set up her medical practice in Los Angeles. Yet, despite the attraction of living and working in a major urban area, Jemison wanted to do something more. She wanted to bring the benefits of modern medicine to people in areas of the world where basic medical care was a critical need. She had done volunteer work in Cuba, Thailand, and Kenya during medical school, so in 1983 she volunteered for the Peace Corps.

Following an intensive training program, Jemison was assigned to the nations of Sierra Leone and Liberia in West Africa as a peace corps medical officer. In addition to supervising health care personnel in hospitals, laboratories, and pharmacies, she wrote self-care manuals and worked with the U.S. Centers for Disease Control on projects aimed at developing a vaccine against the deadly hepatitis B virus.

Jemison spent a total of two and a half years with the peace corps, finally returning to Los Angeles in 1985. Once back in Los Angeles, she went to work for CIGNA Health Plans of California, a health maintenance organization, as a general practitioner. But Jemison was still restless. While with CIGNA, she began graduate classes in engineering. She also resumed her involvement in modern dance, partly for exercise, partly for stress relief, and partly as a type of discipline completely different from the practice of medicine and engineering.

The Astronaut Program

The engineering courses were a step toward another goal that Jemison had set for herself, a goal that would require even more dedication and determination on her part. For years, Jemison had been interested in NASA's astronaut program, but a number of factors had held her back. Neither an American woman nor an African American had flown in space until 1983, when Sally Ride and Guion S. Bluford took their respective shuttle flights. So as a black woman, Jemison had believed that she had little chance of success. As late as 1985 there still had been no African American woman in space, but now Jemison began to think that she had a chance of changing that.

Once she had decided to apply to NASA, Jemison carefully investigated the astronaut program to learn what knowledge might improve her chances of being an astronaut. It was knowing that NASA preferred heavy engineering and science skills in its astronauts that motivated Jemison to take classes in biomedical engineering. She then applied to NASA in the fall of 1985.

Unfortunately for Jemison and her ambitions, the far-reaching effects of the explosion of *Challenger* in January 1986 included a lengthy delay in the astronaut selection process. In 1986, a year after her original application, Jemison applied again and this time was invited to the Johnson Space Center in Houston for interviews and medical exams. Jemison was delighted. She had strong feelings about having a role in the space program. As she noted, space "is the birthright of everyone on this planet. We need to get every group of people in the world involved because it is something that eventually we in the world community are going to have to share."[64]

Once at the Johnson Space Center, Jemison began a period of extensive physical and psychological testing. In addition to intellectual ability and physical fitness, NASA had to be certain that she could endure confinement to the cramped environment of the shuttle.

After the testing and interviews, she returned to her medical practice in Los Angeles to anxiously await NASA's decision. Early in the summer of 1987, Jemison received the call of her dreams. Of two thousand applicants, Jemison was one of fifteen selected for astronaut training. She would be the first African American woman accepted into the U.S. manned spaceflight program.

Although she was now closer than ever to her dream of traveling in space, her year-long training program would be a challenging journey. Jemison trained to be a mission specialist—that is, an astronaut who performs specific experiments while on board the shuttle. Like every crew member, however, she also had to learn the responsibilities of the other astronauts who would be on the mission, including learning how to actually fly the shuttle in the event the pilot became ill or was injured. As part of learning how to fly the shuttle, she practiced by learning how to fly a T-38 trainer jet. Another part of her training would involve a personal obstacle, which was her fear of heights. Several parachute jumps over land and water helped her to gain control over this fear. Other training included studying aerodynamics, physics, meteorology, and one of Jemison's earlier loves, astronomy. She also worked with the communications and navigation systems of the shuttle, again to be prepared in case the astronaut assigned these duties became incapacitated.

Like every astronaut trainee, in order to help her acclimate to the weightlessness of space, Jemison took several rides in the Vomit Comet. Preparing for all contingencies, she and the other astronauts underwent land and water survival training.

One of the most complex elements of the training was working in the shuttle simulator. It is vitally important that each astronaut

Jemison practices parachute jumping, which helped her overcome her fear of heights. The parachute training included jumps over both water and land.

on the mission be able to perform his or her own duties flawlessly, understand the routine duties of the other astronauts, and be prepared to deal with routine procedures as well as any emergency that might occur during a mission. The simulator provided this essential practice.

Finally, in 1988, after countless hours of simulator training, drills, and classroom work, Jemison's name was added to the list of astronauts available for missions. But completing a year's training did not mean she would be immediately assigned to a shuttle flight, and it would be four years before Jemison actually got her opportunity to fly aboard a space shuttle. When her turn came, she would be aboard *Endeavour*.

From Theory to Practice

The mission that Jemison was assigned to, scheduled for the early fall of 1992, would be an eight-day flight in which astronauts from the United States and Japan would work together, performing experiments to study the effects of microgravity on crystals, fluids, and plants, effects that must be understood before travel to other planets can be undertaken.

Jemison would be joined in space by N. Jan Davis and her husband, Mark C. Lee, who would be the first married couple on a mission; Japan's first astronaut, Mamoru Mohri; Jay Apt; Robert L. "Hoot" Gibson; and Curtis L. Brown. These seven *Endeavour* astronauts would be responsible for over forty experiments, ranging from a study of space motion sickness to studying development of fertilized frog eggs in zero gravity.

Because longer space journeys were being contemplated, NASA was becoming more interested in the effects of long-term space travel on the human body. The space agency was particularly concerned with how space travel might affect the

Endeavour's *crew, clockwise from top left: N. Jan Davis, Mark Lee, Robert Gibson, Mae Jemison, Mamoru Mohri, Curtis Brown, and Jay Apt.*

mass and strength of bones. Jemison's research into how men and women lose calcium from their bones and why men experience less loss of bone density than women do during extended periods in space made her a valuable member of the *Endeavour* team.

Finally, all of the preparations had been made for the launch. But there was one more thing that Jemison felt she needed to do before the flight. She telephoned actress Nichelle Nichols, her childhood heroine from *Star Trek*, and made her a promise. Instead of following the NASA-approved procedures for communications, Jemison told Nichols, she would begin each of her shifts with the phrase that Nichols's character, Lieutenant Uhura, spoke each time she reported the status of communications aboard the *Enterprise*: "*Hailing frequencies open.*"

Endeavour's Journey

On September 12, 1992, the *Endeavour* crew went through the same preflight procedure that they had practiced countless times. This time, however, instead of walking away from a simulator at the end of a work day, the seven astronauts strapped themselves into their seats and rode *Endeavour* into space.

Once in orbit, each astronaut was busy with assigned duties. In one of her assigned experiments, Jemison tried using a technique called biofeedback to fight the symptoms of space sickness. Biofeedback involves harnessing the human mind to consciously control some bodily functions. For example, with practice a person can gain control over such automatic functions as breathing and heartbeat. Jemison speculated that this method would be successful in fighting the nausea, known as space sickness, that often accompanies weightlessness.

Although the astronauts' days were filled with experiments and routine maintenance duties, they also had free time. Jemison spent some of her spare time observing the continuously changing panorama outside the shuttle window. Dancing to her favorite music was not possible in zero gravity, so Jemison settled for listening to some of her favorite recording artists, such as Aretha Franklin and Stevie Wonder.

Finally, after eight days in space, it was time to return to Earth. The astronauts did the necessary "housekeeping" such as securing loose items before reentering earth's gravity. When the shuttle landed, the astronauts were all given physical exams before they disembarked. Other than feeling heavy and out of

Endeavour *lands after an eight-day mission. In speeches, Jemison used her experience aboard* Endeavour *to encourage children to work hard to achieve their dreams.*

balance, normal symptoms after eight days in orbit, the doctor pronounced the astronauts fit and allowed them to exit the shuttle.

A Space-age Role Model

In the months following her flight, Jemison made many personal appearances, including celebrations in Chicago in conjunction with her thirty-sixth birthday on October 17. In addition to sharing with audiences her experiences as an astronaut, she had advice for young people, especially minorities and children from poor families. Jemison wanted her experience as a successful African American woman to inspire children to succeed, regardless of their ethnicity: "Don't let anyone rob you of your imagination, your creativity, or your curiosity. It's your place in the world and it's your life. Go and do all you can with it, and make it the life you want to live."[65]

Life After NASA

During her six years at NASA, Jemison had proven that hard work and determination could pay off, a point she wanted to make with young people, but she felt it was time for a new phase in her life. She asked herself, "Do I get only one opportunity, and do I have to keep it for life. Because something was once exactly right for me, does that mean I cannot grow and change?"[66] Jemison had worked hard to fulfill her obligations to the space program. She understood that a great deal of money had been spent on her training, but after a time she began to feel confined by the rigid environment at NASA, where tasks were repetitious and controlled. She wanted to work somewhere she felt she had more opportunity for creativity, an environment more open than NASA's.

As a first step toward a new career, Jemison took a leave of absence from NASA to teach a course called "Space Age Technology in Developing Countries" at Dartmouth College in Hanover, New Hampshire. Finally, in the spring of 1993, Jemison decided to resign from NASA. "Mae's personality was too big for [a career at NASA]," says Homer Heckman, her training manager for the *Endeavour* mission. Although he described Jemison's 1993 resignation from NASA as amicable, he acknowledged that her resignation represented a loss to the space agency. "NASA had spent a lot of money training her; she also filled a niche, obviously, being a woman of color."[67]

Jemison wanted to use some of the advanced technologies she had mastered while working at NASA to improve the lives of people in underdeveloped nations. She formed her own consulting firm, the Jemison Group, to work toward that goal. Employing a select staff of experts in a variety of skills and technologies, the Jemison Group develops electricity-generating systems that employ solar power and then puts them

One of the Jemison Group's projects was a satellite communications system.

to use in countries that do not have adequate sources of electricity. The group's energy generators are based on environmental responsibility, using renewable resources such as the Sun's energy to fuel generating plants. In addition, the company developed a satellite communications system, ALAFIYA (a Yoruba word meaning "good health"), to help improve health care for people living in West Africa.

In addition to using space-age technology to help remote regions and developing nations, Jemison works with students from around the world. She started the Earth We Share international science camp, where students ages twelve to sixteen work together to solve current global dilemmas, such as determining Earth's population capacity, and examine economic issues, including predicting which public stocks will be booming in the year 2030. Now in its sixth year, the four-week residential program is free to all participants and builds critical-thinking and problem-solving skills through an experimental curriculum.

In addition to her work with young people, Jemison serves as director of the Jemison Institute for Advancing Technology in Developing Countries, based at Dartmouth College. The institute has organized roundtable discussion groups composed of experts in many fields to brainstorm an economic, technological, and political framework for cooperative energy development between the United States and African countries.

She is also a professor of environmental studies at Dartmouth College, where she teaches a course titled "Technology and Sustainable Development." In this course, students learn skills of applying satellite communications and other technologies to improving health and quality of life in developing countries.

Other Frontiers

Jemison continues to add a wide variety of experiences to her repertoire, dividing her time between New Hampshire, where she teaches spring semester classes at Dartmouth, and Houston, where she directs the Jemison Group, as well as traveling, lecturing, and appearing in a variety of educational programs on cable and on public television.

Jemison's busy career and volunteer work show no signs of slowing, and she continues to use modern dance for exercise and stress relief. It is difficult for those meeting her for the first time to believe that this youthful-looking woman has already experienced such a diversity of careers as medical doctor, astronaut, college professor, environmentalist, and businesswoman. Still only in her forties, Mae Jemison may yet conquer new frontiers.

NOTES

Introduction: The Trailblazers

1. Quoted in Michael Collins, *Liftoff: The Story of America's Adventure in Space.* New York: Grove, 1988, p. 45.

2. Quoted in Collins, *Liftoff*, p. 45.

Chapter 1: Man in Space: From Watcher to Wanderer

3. Quoted in William E. Burrows, *Exploring Space: Voyages in the Solar System and Beyond.* New York: Random House, 1990, p. 25.

4. Quoted in Burrows, *Exploring Space*, p. 69.

5. Quoted in Peter R. Bond, *Heroes in Space: From Gagarin to Challenger.* New York: Basil Blackwell, 1987, p. 139.

6. Quoted in Richard Lewis, *The Voyages of "Apollo 11": The Exploration of the Moon.* New York: New York Times Book, 1974, p. 159.

Chapter 2: Yuri Gagarin: The Columbus of the Cosmos

7. Quoted in Gene and Clare Gurney, *Cosmonauts in Orbit: The Story of the Soviet Manned Space Program.* Oxford, UK: Basil Blackwell, 1987, p. 9.

8. Quoted in Bond, *Heroes in Space*, p. 13.

9. Quoted in ALLSTAR Network, "Yuri A. Gagarin." www.allstar. fiu.edu/aerojava/gagarin.htm.

10. Quoted in Bond, *Heroes in Space*, p. 14.

11. Quoted in James Oburg, "Celebrating Gagarin's Anniversary." http://solar.rtd.utk.edu/~mwade/articles/celrsary.htm.

12. Quoted in Shirley Thomas, *Men of Space.* Philadelphia: Chilton, 1961, p. 113.

13. Quoted in Gurney, *Cosmonauts in Orbit*, p. 15.

14. Quoted in Bond, *Heroes in Space*, pp. 15–16.

15. Bond, *Heroes in Space*, p. 12.

16. Quoted in Bond, *Heroes in Space*, p. 17.

17. Quoted in Peter Smolders, *Soviets in Space.* New York: Tapplinger, 1974, p. 116.

18. Quoted in *New Scientist*, "Fallen Hero," April 1998, Archive 25. www. newscientist.com/ns/980425/review.html.

19. Quoted in Bond, *Heroes in Space*, p. 17.

20. Quoted in John F. Graham, *Space Explorations: from Talisman of the Past to Gateway for the Future.* http://www.space.edu/projects/book/chapter20.html.

Chapter 3: John Glenn: Grandpa in Space

21. Quoted in Frank Van Riper, *Glenn: The Astronaut Who Would Be President.* New York: Empire Books, 1983, p. 157.

22. Van Riper, *Glenn*, p. 155.

23. Quoted in Van Riper, *Glenn*, p. 157.

24. Quoted in Bond, *Heroes in Space*, p. 41.

25. Quoted in Bond, *Heroes in Space*, p. 42.

26. Quoted in STS-95 Educational Downlink, October 31, 1998. www.shuttle-STS-95/transcripts/fd3edutranscript.htm.

Chapter 4: Neil Armstrong: A Giant Leap for Mankind

27. Quoted in *New York Times*, "*Gemini 8* Astronauts Forced Down in West Pacific After Docking in Space," March 17, 1966, p. 20.

28. Quoted in *Dayton Journal Herald*, "Moon Was Dream to Shy Armstrong," July 11, 1969, p. 14.

29. Quoted in Lawrence Mosher, "Neil Armstrong: From the Start He Aimed for the Moon," *National Observer*, July 7, 1967.

30. Quoted in Neil Armstrong, Michael Collins, and Edwin Aldrin Jr., *First on the Moon: A Voyage with Neil Armstrong, Michael Collins, And Edwin Aldrin.* Boston: Little, Brown, 1970, p. 115.

31. Neil Armstrong, "The Men Write About Themselves and What They Are Doing Now," *Life*, September 27, 1963, p. 84.

32. Quoted in Armstrong, Collins, and Aldrin, *First on the Moon*, p. 27.

33. Quoted in Bond, *Heroes in Space*, p. 190.

34. Quoted in Bond, *Heroes in Space*, p. 191.

35. Quoted in Bond, *Heroes in Space*, p. 198.

36. Quoted in Edgar Cartwright, ed., *Apollo Expeditions to the Moon.* Washington, DC: National Aeronautics and Space Administration, 1975, p. 215.

37. Quoted in Bond, *Heroes in Space*, p. 200.

38. Quoted in Matthew Purdy, "In Rural Ohio, Armstrong Lives on His Own Dark Side of the Moon," *New York Times*, July 20, 1994, p. A14.

Chapter 5: Sally Ride: Breaking the Barriers

39. Quoted in Jerry Alden, "Sally Ride: Ready for Liftoff," *Newsweek*, June 13, 1983, p. 45.

40. Quoted in Frederick Golden, "Sally's Joy Ride into the Sky," *Time*, June 13, 1983, p. 57.

41. Quoted in National Women's Hall of Fame, "The Women of the Hall: Sally Ride." www.greatwomen.org/ride.htm.

42. Quoted in Bond, *Heroes in Space*, p. 410.

43. Quoted in Mark Carreau, "Sally Ride Is Leaving NASA." www.chron.com/content/interactive/space/archives/87/870921.htm.

44. Quoted in Carreau, "Sally Ride Is Leaving NASA."

45. Quoted in NASA Watch, "Space.com Names Dr. Sally Ride to the Board of Directors," June 29, 1999. www.reston.com/nasa/space.com/06.29.99.ride.space.com.html.

46. Quoted in Fred Burning, "A Ticket to a Boring Sally Ride," *Maclean's*, July 25, 1983.

Chapter 6: Christa McAuliffe: The Teacher and the Dream

47. Quoted in Robert T. Hohler, *"I Touch the Future—": The Story of Christa McAuliffe*. New York: Random House, 1986, p. 22.

48. Quoted in Charlene W. Billings, *Christa McAuliffe: Pioneer Space Teacher*. Hillside, NJ: Enslow, 1986, p. 18.

49. Quoted in Hohler, *"I Touch the Future—"*, p. 37.

50. Quoted in Hohler, *"I Touch the Future—"*, p. 29.

51. Quoted in Hohler, *"I Touch the Future—"*, p. 37.

52. Quoted in Grace George Corrigan, *A Journal for Christa*. Lincoln: University of Nebraska Press, 1993, p. 43.

53. Quoted in Hohler, *"I Touch the Future—"*, p. 54.

54. Quoted in Billings, *Christa McAuliffe*, p. 24.

55. Quoted in Billings, *Christa McAuliffe*, p. 23.

56. Quoted in Hohler, *"I Touch the Future—"*, p. 14.

57. Quoted in Hohler, *"I Touch the Future—"*, p. 14.

58. Quoted in Hohler, *"I Touch the Future—"*, pp. 170–71.

59. Quoted in Henry S. F. Cooper Jr., *Before Liftoff: The Making of a Space Shuttle Crew*. Baltimore: Johns Hopkins University Press, 1987, p. 249.

60. Theresa Bruni, interview with author. Houston, TX, October, 1999.

61. Quoted in Hohler, "*I Touch the Future—*", p. 260.

Chapter 7: Mae Jemison: Exploring Space and Serving Humankind

62. Quoted in Jesse Katz, "Mae Jemison: Shooting Star," *Stanford Today*, July/August 1996. www.stanford.edu/dept/news/stanford today/ed/9607/9607mj01.shtml.

63. Quoted in Katz, "Mae Jemison."

64. Quoted in National Women's Hall of Fame, "The Women of the Hall: Mae Jemison." www.greatwomen.org/jemison.htm.

65. Quoted in National Science Foundation, "World Class Science Stars: Mae Jemison." www.nsf.gov.od/lpa/nstw/kids/cards/world/mae.htm.

66. Quoted in Diane Manuel, "Jemison Brings Message of Hope to Grads," *Stanford Today*, July/August 1996. www.stanford. edu/dept/news/stanfordtoday/ed/9607/9607ncf201.shtml.

67. Quoted in Katz, "Mae Jemison."

1903

December 12—Orville Wright makes a twelve-second flight in a motorized flying machine in Kitty Hawk, North Carolina.

1957

In the fall, the Soviet Union launches *Sputnik I*, a 184-pound, basketball-shaped artificial satellite.

November 3—Laike the dog is launched by the Soviet Union to become the first animal in space.

1958

January 1—The United States launches its first artificial satellite.

April 2—Formation of the National Aeronautics and Space Administration (NASA) is proposed by President Dwight D. Eisenhower.

October 1—The first day of operations for NASA.

December 12—A squirrel monkey, Old Reliable, is launched into space by the United States.

1959

March 3—The United States sends *Pioneer 4* to the Moon. The first U.S. lunar flyby occurs.

April—NASA selects the astronauts for the Mercury missions: Alan B. Shepard, John H. Glenn Jr., L. Gordon Cooper, Walter M. Shirra, M. Scott Carpenter, Virgil I. "Gus" Grissom, and Donald K. "Deke" Slayton.

May 28—A rhesus monkey, Abel, is launched into space by the United States.

September 12—The Soviet Union launches *Lunik II*, the first man-made object to land on the moon's surface.

1960

April 1—The United States launches *Tiros I*, the first successful weather satellite.

1961

April 12—Soviet cosmonaut Yuri Gagarin rides *Vostok 1* to become the first man in space.

May 5—U.S. astronaut Alan Shepard becomes the first American in space aboard *Freedom 7*.

July 21—Gus Grissom becomes the second American in space aboard *Liberty Bell 7*. *Liberty Bell 7* is lost under three miles of ocean water when a side hatch blows prematurely before the capsule can be recovered; Grissom is safely rescued.

1962

February 2—John Glenn becomes the first American to orbit Earth.

1963

June 16—Soviet cosmonaut Valentina Tereshkovae becomes the first woman in space.

1967

January 27—Gus Grissom, Roger Chaffee, and Edwin White die in a launch-pad fire during testing of the *Apollo 1* rocket.

April 4—Soviet cosmonaut Vladimir Komarov is the first person to die during an actual space mission.

1969

July 20—U.S. astronaut Neil Armstrong is the first man to walk on the Moon during the Apollo 11 mission.

1970

April 13—Fifty-five hours and fifty-five minutes into the Apollo 13 lunar mission, a service module oxygen tank ruptures. The lunar mission is aborted and, after many anxious hours, astronauts James A. Lovell Jr., John L. Swigert Jr., and Fred W. Haise Jr. are safely returned to Earth on April 14.

1973

May 14—America's first space station, Skylab I, is launched into orbit.

May 25—Charles Conrad Jr., Paul J. Weitz, and Joseph P. Kerwin fly the first manned mission to Skylab I.

1975

July 17—A U.S. *Apollo* spacecraft and the Soviet Union's *Soyuz* spacecraft dock in space, the first joint U.S.-Soviet mission.

1981

April 12—The first space shuttle, *Columbia*, is launched by the United States. On board are astronauts John W. Young and Robert L. Crippen.

1983

June 18—Sally Ride becomes the first American woman in space aboard the space shuttle *Challenger*.

August 30—Guion S. Bluford rides the *Challenger* to become the first African American in space.

1986

January 28—The *Challenger* explodes seventy-three seconds into its mission, and the seven-astronaut crew perishes. On board were Christa McAuliffe, Ronald McNair, Ellison Onizuka, Judith Resnick, Richard Scobee, and Michael Smith.

February 19—The core of Russia's Mir space station is launched.

February 20—The first element of the Soviet Union's Mir space station is launched.

1998

December 4—Mission STS-88 is launched. The purpose of this mission is to connect the U.S.-built Node 1 space station element with the functional energy block. This is the first element of the international space station.

December 10—Soviet cosmonaut Sergei Krikalev and U.S. astronaut Robert Cabana open the hatch between the shuttle *Endeavour* and the first element of the international space station.

FOR FURTHER READING

Charlene W. Billings, *Christa McAuliffe: Pioneer Space Teacher*. Hillside, NJ: Enslow, 1986. Describes the life of this New Hampshire schoolteacher before the teacher-in-space fame. A comprehensive description of astronaut training is given along with details of the explosion of the space shuttle *Challenger*.

Carolyn Blacknell, *Sally Ride: America's First Woman in Space*. Minneapolis: Dillon, 1984. This biography covers the childhood, education, and astronaut career of the first American woman in space. Coverage is also given to Ride's successful career after the fame of being America's first woman astronaut.

Carmen Bresden, *Neil Armstrong: A Space Biography*. Springfield, NJ: Enslow, 1998. This biography takes the reader through Armstrong's childhood, military career, and his experiences as the first man on the moon. After his astronaut career, the biography follows private citizen Armstrong's efforts to remove himself from the limelight.

Liza Burby, *Mae Jemison: The First African-American Woman Astronaut*. New York: PowerKids, 1997. An African American, from a middle-class background, Mae Jemison's meteoric rise to a successful career in medicine, followed by the nationwide fame of being the first African American woman in space, is described in this biography.

Michael Cassutt, *Who's Who in Space: The First Twenty-Five Years*. Boston: GK Hall, 1987. In addition to U.S. and Soviet astronauts, engineers and scientists get a fair share of coverage in this volume.

Michael D. Cole, *"Vostok 1": First Human in Space*. Springfield, NJ: Enslow, 1995. The life, career, and death of the first human being to be sent into space is described in this biography. Yuri Gagarin's military career, preparations for his launch, his observations from space, and his untimely death as he trained to return to the cosmonaut corps are well-detailed through words and photographs.

Chris Crocker, *Great American Astronauts*. New York: Franklin Watts, 1988. The lives and careers of ten well-known astronauts are highlighted. Also includes some firsts in the U.S. space program.

Edward F. Dolan, *Famous Firsts in Space*. New York: Cobblehill Books, 1989. Events chronicled include the first satellite launched by the Soviet Union, the Soviet Union's victory in putting the first man into space, the first space walk, the first man on the moon, and the first shuttle flights.

Additional Works Consulted

Books

Neil Armstrong, Michael Collins, and Edwin E. Aldrin Jr., *First on the Moon: A Voyage with Neil Armstrong, Michael Collins, and Edwin Aldrin*. Boston: Little, Brown, 1970. The doors of the space agency are opened to the reader in this first-person plural narrative. In addition to their work with NASA, personal family incidents are also shared by the *Apollo 11* astronauts.

Peter R. Bond, *Heroes in Space: From Gagarin to* Challenger. New York: Basil Blackwell, 1987. Begins with brief tracing of the work of pioneer scientists and engineers of the space program. From a well-detailed account of Gagarin's landing in a farmer's field, narrative carries through the *Challenger* tragedy of 1986.

William E. Burrows, *Exploring Space: Voyages in the Solar System and Beyond*. New York: Random House, 1990. Beginning with Galileo's idea that humans could theoretically travel to the Moon, the philosophies of the "watchers" and the "wanderers" of space are well described.

Edgar Cartwright, ed., *Apollo Expeditions to the Moon*. Washington, DC: National Aeronautics and Space Administration, 1975. Individual chapters are authored by noted experts in the American space program, including Robert Gilruth and Wernher von Braun. Generously illustrated and diagrammed.

Andrew Chaikin, *A Man on the Moon: The Voyages of the Apollo Astronauts*. New York: Penguin Putnam, 1994. A comprehensive narrative of the Apollo missions, from liftoff to lunar touchdown to reentry. From the tragic beginnings of the *Apollo 1* launch-pad fire, the missions are chronicled through the splashdown of *Apollo 11*.

Michael Collins, *Liftoff: The Story of America's Adventure in Space*. New York: Grove, 1988. A fairly comprehensive journal of U.S. manned spaceflight emphasizing *Apollo 11* but with references to the Mercury, Gemini, and other Apollo missions. Also includes details on Skylab, Apollo-Soyuz, and the space shuttles. The acronyms and key terms directory is a useful feature.

Henry S. F. Cooper Jr., *Before Liftoff: The Making of a Space Shuttle Crew*. Baltimore: Johns Hopkins University Press, 1987. A well-detailed journal of astronaut training, dating from November 1983 to October 1984.

Grace George Corrigan, *A Journal for Christa*. Lincoln: University of Nebraska Press, 1993. Corrigan journals the life of her daughter, teacher-astronaut Christa McAuliffe, from Christa's childhood through the explosion of the *Challenger* space shuttle, which claimed the lives of McAuliffe and six other astronauts.

Henry C. Dethloff, *Suddenly Tomorrow Came: A History of the Johnson Space Center*. Washington, DC: National Aeronautics and Space Administration, 1993. Describes the idealized beginnings of the U.S. space program and the problem-plagued period following the *Challenger* disaster.

Tim Furniss, *Manned Space Flight Log*. London: Jane's, 1983. A good source of statistics from Gagarin's flight through the 101st manned spaceflight.

Gene and Clare Gurney, *Cosmonauts in Orbit: The Story of the Soviet Manned Space Program*. Oxford, UK: Basil Blackwell, 1987. Traces the history of manned and unmanned Soviet missions. One of the better accounts of the early life of Yuri Gagarin.

Robert T. Hohler, *"I Touch the Future—": The Story of Christa McAuliffe*. New York: Random House, 1986. Published after the deaths of the seven *Challenger* astronauts, the author has created a three-dimensional picture of the life of teacher-astronaut Christa McAuliffe, giving equal emphasis to admirable qualities and to character quirks that annoyed some friends and family.

Robert D. Lanius, *Frontiers of Space Exploration*. Westport, CT: Greenwood, 1998. A chronology and overview of space exploration. Includes dialogue from the transmissions of the Apollo 11 mission.

Richard Lewis, *The Voyages of "Apollo 11": The Exploration of the Moon*. New York: The New York Times Book, 1974. A good chronicle of the Apollo missions.

Peter Smolders, *Soviets in Space*. New York: Tapplinger, 1974. Highlight the history of the Soviet space program.

Shirley Thomas, *Men of Space*. Philadelphia: Chilton, 1961. Provides profiles of leaders in space research and exploration.

Frank Van Riper, *Glenn: The Astronaut Who Would Be President*. New York: Empire Books, 1983. Takes John Glenn through four careers: military pilot, astronaut, politician, and businessman. Candid anecdotes from friends give a realistic view of where the legend leaves off and the man begins.

Periodicals

Jerry Alden, "Sally Ride: Ready for Liftoff," *Newsweek*, June 13, 1983.

Neil Armstrong, "The Men Write About Themselves and What They Are Doing Now," *Life*, September 27, 1963.

Fred Burning, "A Ticket to a Boring Sally Ride," *Maclean's*, July 25, 1983.

Dayton Journal Herald, "Moon Was a Dream to Shy Armstrong," July 11, 1969.

Frederick Golden, "Sally's Joy Ride into the Sky," *Time*, June 13, 1983.

Lawrence Mosher, "Neil Armstrong: From the Start He Aimed for the Moon," *National Observer*, July 7, 1969.

New York Times, "*Gemini 8* Astronauts Forced Down in West Pacific After Docking in Space," March 17, 1966.

Matthew Purdy, "In Rural Ohio, Armstrong Quietly Lives on His Own Dark Side of the Moon," *New York Times*, July 20, 1994.

Internet Sources

ALLSTAR Network, "Yuri A. Gagarin." www.allstar.fiu.edu/aerojava/gagarin.htm.

Mark Carreau, "Sally Ride Is Leaving NASA." www.chron.com/content/interactive/space/archives/87/870921.html.

Florida Today Space Online, April 23, 1998. Old-man-in-space Jokes Amuse John Glenn. www.flatoday.com/space/explore/stories/1998/042398i.htm.

Jesse Katz, "Mae Jemison: Shooting Star," *Stanford Today*, July/August 1996. www.stanford.edu/dept/news/stanfordtoday/ed/9607/9607mj01.shtml.

Diane Manuel, "Jemison Brings Message of Hope to Grads," *Stanford Today*, July/August 1996. www.stanford.edu/dept/news/stanfordtoday/ed/9607/9607ncf201.shtml.

NASA Watch, "Space.com Names Dr. Sally Ride to the Board of Directors," June 29, 1999. www.reston.com/nasa/space.com/06.29.99.ride.space.com.html.

National Science Foundation, "World Class Science Stars: Mae Jemison." www.nsf.gov/od/1pa/nstw/kids/cards/world/mae.htm.

National Women's Hall of Fame, "The Women of the Hall: Mae Jemison." www.greatwomen.org/jemison.htm.

———, "The Women of the Hall: Sally Ride." www.greatwomen.org/ride.htm.

New Scientist, "Fallen Hero," April 1998, Archive 25. www.newscientist.com/ns/980425/review.html.

James Oburg, "Celebrating Gagarin's Anniversary." http://solar.rtd.utk.edu/~mwade/articles/celrsary.htm.

STS-95 Educational Downlink, October 31, 1998. *Discovery* Comes Home. www.shuttle.nasa.gov/shuttle/archives/sts-95/

Ultimate Space Place, "Friendship 7." www.thespaceplace.com/history/mercury/mercury06.html.

INDEX

PICTURE CREDITS

ABOUT THE AUTHOR

Sheila Wyborny is a retired science and social studies teacher. She lives in Houston, Texas with her husband. They spend their leisure time flying and visiting areas of historical interest.